MW01285462

Who Are These People Anyway?

The Iroquois and Their Neighbors

Christopher Vecsey, *Series Editor*

Who Are These People Anyway?

CHIEF IRVING POWLESS JR.
OF THE
ONONDAGA NATION

Edited by Lesley Forrester

Syracuse University Press

Cover and title page: Wampum reproduction and photograph by Darren Bonaparte.

Copyright © 2016 by Syracuse University Press
Syracuse, New York 13244-5290

All Rights Reserved

First Edition 2016
17 18 19 20 21   6 5 4 3 2

∞ The paper used in this publication meets the minimum requirements
of the American National Standard for Information Sciences—Permanence
of Paper for Printed Library Materials, ANSI Z39.48-1992.

For a listing of books published and distributed by Syracuse University Press,
visit www.SyracuseUniversityPress.syr.edu.

ISBN: 978-0-8156-3449-2 (cloth)   978-0-8156-1070-0 (paperback)
978-0-8156-5373-8 (e-book)

Library of Congress Cataloging-in-Publication Data
Names: Powless, Irving, author. | Forrester, Lesley, editor.
Title: Who are these people anyway? / Chief Irving Powless Jr. of the
    Onondaga Nation ; edited by Lesley Forrester.
Description: Syracuse, New York : Syracuse University Press, [2016] |
    Series: The Iroquois and their neighbors
Identifiers: LCCN 2015045711| ISBN 9780815634492 (cloth : alk. paper) |
    ISBN 9780815610700 (pbk. : alk. paper) | ISBN 9780815653738 (e-book)
Subjects: LCSH: Powless, Irving. | Iroquois philosophy. | Onondaga
    Indians—New York (State) | Iroquois Indians—Government relations.
    United States—Civilization. | Onondaga Indians—New York
    (State)—Biography. | Onondaga Indians—New York (State)—History. |
    Indians, Treatment of—New York (State)—History. | Whites—New York
    (State)—Relations with Indians. | Indian philosophy—New York (State)
Classification: LCC E99.I7 P69 2016 | DDC 974.7004/97554—dc23 LC
record available at http://lccn.loc.gov/2015045711

Manufactured in the United States of America

Dedicated to my wife, Helen,
who taught me how to be a human being

Statement read when conferring upon Chief Irving Powless Jr. an honorary doctor of laws degree from Syracuse University:

Irving Powless, Jr., Chief of the Beaver Clan and secretary of the Onondaga Nation, author, historian, ambassador, actor, musician, veteran, defender of the environment, champion of justice, you embody the wisdom of centuries. As a key spokesperson for the Haudenosaunee nations, you have opened the minds of many to self-determination rights.

You wear the mantle of leadership with profound dignity and generosity of spirit, having meticulously researched the foundations of legal and political relations between the Haudenosaunee people and the United States and having patiently educated generations of leaders about the implications of sovereignty. It was [from] your letter to then-President of the United States Richard Nixon that pivotal legal decisions cascaded, establishing the principle that New York State could not collect taxes on Indian land.

We are honored to recognize you today for your fortitude and sage statesmanship, as well as your tireless efforts in cultural preservation and responsible environment[al] stewardship that set an example for all nations to follow.

May 10, 2009

Nancy Cantor
Former Chancellor and President
Syracuse University

Contents

Preface

It has been my great honor, particularly as a non-Indigenous woman, to have earned the trust of Chief Powless, in order to work with him so closely on this book.

Award-winning Mohawk journalist, Douglas George (Kanentiio), had originally approached me about the book after reading *And Grandma Said . . . Iroquois Teachings as Passed Down through the Oral Tradition* by Tom Porter. Doug liked the oral history approach of that book, where I had transcribed Tom's speeches and edited them into a written document. He felt it was important for other Haudenosaunee elders to get their own teachings into print in a similar way.

Unbeknownst to me until we met, Chief Powless was not at all convinced, at first, that a book was a good idea. And the book he thought he might like to write was very different from what I had expected. He decided to begin by dictating the sections that ask, "Who are these people anyway?" As he will explain, his people have been asking this question about the newcomers from their earliest contact.

Also since those early days, non-Indigenous writers, especially anthropologists, have been analyzing the Haudenosaunee in minute detail. This has mostly been done as dispassionately as one might study bugs in a dusty museum case. Such analysis has failed to portray accurately the living, spiritually-vital, and democratic people they are—a people with one of the most complex language systems in the world. It was finally time, in the chief's opinion, to turn things around and subject the newcomers to some analysis. Sometimes gently tongue-in-cheek, sometimes scathing, this analysis is a natural response, in my view, to these centuries of stereotyping and misunderstanding.

When we began, in the fall of 2009, Chief Powless would dictate each section that asked the question, "Who are these people anyway?" When he had finished dictating for the day, he would make sure that all my recording equipment was turned off. Only then would he tell me the wonderful stories about his people and his life that I had expected to be the most important parts of this book.

I kept encouraging him to consider allowing me to transcribe these stories. I had two goals and two audiences in mind. My first goal was for the chief to tell us newcomers about his own culture as seen through his own eyes. How else could the Haudenosaunee be more accurately described than by one of their own people, especially one who has lived his traditions for over eight decades? The other goal was to document for future generations of Haudenosaunee, on paper, his vital knowledge of the old ways, and particularly his knowledge about the treaties.

As someone raised in the oral tradition, Chief Powless was not particularly attracted to the idea of writing all of this down in a book, at first. He had already passed on his knowledge and his stories in the traditional manner. However, as we got to know each other better, he gradually consented to having the equipment turned on as he dictated treaty details and the personal anecdotes that have brought the work alive for me. Over many months of dictation and discussion, both of us have often commented on how much we have enjoyed this process.

So the reader may find that at times Chief Powless is addressing the newcomers, and at other times he is addressing future generations of his own people who have not had the opportunity to learn about themselves through the oral tradition.

Perhaps a few words on punctuation and syntax might be helpful to readers. The tendency in English is for the speaker to report the comments of others—especially those comments that came to them indirectly—by means of a subordinate clause. For example, "He looked from the east shore of Lake Oneida, looked west, and said . . . *that he thought he would build an empire.*" However, the oral tradition is much more about bringing as much of a sense of immediacy to a story or event as possible. In this way, the retelling reanimates—or we could even say "re-inspirits"—the event, breathing life back into it as if it is happening now. Listeners can feel they are present while historical or sacred events are relived in the present moment.

Therefore, in order to maintain this sense of being present, I have opted to preserve Chief Powless's literal dictation in these situations, rather than to use the conventions of mainstream culture. For example: "He looked from the east shore of Lake Oneida, looked west, and said, '*I think I'll build an empire.*'" When he was quoting other people, I transcribed the words as direct quotes, regardless of whether the chief's knowledge of the words was through personal contact (e.g., quoting his cousin Oren Lyons) or through oral history (e.g., quoting George Washington). For the author's views on this process, the reader may want to look at the chapter, "We were there."

To use the more formal description of one writer on the subject, "[o]ral history is also good at restoring pivotal moments to life, at helping us imagine the drama of impending decisions and their unimaginable consequences, as distinct from the all-too-familiar monuments these decisions become in the landscape of the historical past tense."[*]

It is my humble hope that I have been able to transcribe and edit Chief Powless's dictations into a book in a way that does his spoken words justice. It would have been impossible to complete the book without the invaluable help of three people.

The first is Dr. Robert W. Venables, the history professor whom Chief Powless mentions several times in the book. It has been a privilege to observe the deep and profound friendship these two have shared since 1971 and the tireless dedication of Dr. Venables to jointly uncovering the true history of the Haudenosaunee. His help with the manuscript has been invaluable.

The second is Jay Eugene Meacham (Ganeñ'do·doñ'), supervisor of Ne' Eñhadiweññayeñde·'nha' (the Onondaga Language Center), who provided the correct spelling of the Onondaga words and phrases. He was

---

[*] Michael Frisch, "Oral History, Documentary, and the Mystification of Power," in *A Shared Authority: Essays on the Craft and Meaning of Oral and Public History* (Albany: State Univ. of New York Press, 1990), 163.

able to fulfill Chief Powless's request to use as much of the orthography of Audrey Shenandoah (Goñwaiani) as possible. Goñwaiani, a beloved Onondaga clan mother, passed on during the writing of the book, so there is a mix of the two orthographies used: that of a respected clan mother who was the chief's dear friend, and that used by Meacham and more contemporary Onondaga linguists.

The third is Doug George (Kanentiio) whose idea it was to write the book in the first place. Without his enthusiasm and encouragement, the book would never have gotten off the ground.

I am also grateful that, as a non-Indigenous person, I was made so welcome by the people of Onondaga and by the chief's family. I particularly enjoyed meeting his grandchildren.

If some of the chief's descriptions of American politics and some of the fun he pokes at non-Native people begin to rub some readers the wrong way, they can only begin to imagine how much more difficult centuries of misunderstanding—and intentional mistreatment—have been for the Haudenosaunee, and indeed for the rest of the Indigenous world.

After almost twenty years of listening to and transcribing the words of Haudenosaunee elders, it is clear to me that their oral tradition is characterized by a considerable amount of repetition. Topics of importance that need to be emphasized and well-understood are repeated over and over, with almost infinite variations suited to the occasion or to the current audience. In contrast, a common non-Native expression is, "I've already heard that before." In the fast-paced mainstream culture, the implication is that nothing is worth hearing twice.

But in Indian Country there is an awareness, only recently acknowledged by non-Native adult educators, that humans need to hear things again and again until we are able to grasp their impact not just with our heads, but also with our hearts. This kind of repetition could be compared to the way non-Native people expect musicians and singers to perform their favorite music repeatedly, allowing the song to affect them much more deeply than a single exposure might.

Repeated listening to Chief Powless's incisive descriptions of historical events, treaties, and court decisions will etch details into memory. And listening to his repetition of environmental and spiritual matters will bring home his love of all parts of creation in ways that can strengthen our own.

I hope you will enjoy this book as much as I have enjoyed working on it.

October 2015

Lesley Forrester
Editor

Introduction

I, Irving Powless Jr., known as Tsaʔdegaihwadeʔ, am telling the stories and events in this book to illustrate to readers that we, as Haudenosaunee people, have our own way of thinking that is very different from the white people. We don't understand a lot of the things that they do. And that's why we ask the question, "Who are these people anyway?"

Who Are These People Anyway?

Greetings

Nyaweñha sgeñ·noñʔ.

I have greeted you in the language of the Onondagas and I have thanked the Creator that we are all well and that we are able to gather together today.

Probably I should identify myself

Numerous people where I've lectured have told me that they think I should publish some of my stories. So this is an attempt to do that.

But in order to inform the reader who has not been at my lectures or who doesn't know who I am, probably I should identify myself. I am Chief Dehatgahdoñs, chief of the Beaver Clan of the Onondaga Nation. I've been sitting in this position since 1964.

My English name is Irving Powless Jr. And I've resided here at Onondaga for more than eighty years. I was born September 4, 1929.

My grandfather, Welcome, lived across the road from here, from where I live now. He lived with my grandmother, Phoebe. Phoebe was Onondaga. Welcome was Oneida. He was a very industrious man. He had a team of horses and he plowed all over the place. He farmed and he raised my father and my father's brothers and sister.

My father, born in 1905, started school in 1910. In 1915 he was all done with school. He went to the fourth grade. That was it. And because of Depression time, my father didn't have a job, didn't have a place to stay. So when he got married, he moved in with his father and mother.

And that's where I was born. And so the first few years of my life, I spent gardening with my grandfather. Every morning we would go down and we would put the team of horses together. And we'd go out to the gardens and we would plow, weed, harvest, and so forth, depending on what was the time of the season.

But because my grandfather was still using the farm, my father and his brothers had no place to farm for their families. So, since my father had learned how to speak English, this enabled him to go down into the city of Syracuse and get a job and work down there.

Now that he had a job, he had some money to pay rent. So we moved out of my grandparents' house. And because the jobs that were available were in the city of Syracuse, he decided to move off the territory into a neighboring town called Nedrow.

So he and my uncles worked in the coal yards down in the city. Bill and my father worked at Kelly's. And then my Uncle Wilmer worked at Amos—Amos Coal Yard. They carried coal. And that's what our people were: laborers. We were out digging ditches and so forth. We ended up building the buildings. We were ironworkers and construction workers. And we didn't need an education to construct or dig a ditch. So our people survived.

And my dad got a house there in Nedrow. And there he could ride a trolley car from where we lived to his work. And he did that for about a year. Then he found a place that was just a few blocks away from where he worked. And we moved down there. We lived there for a couple of years. Then after a couple of years, we moved to another place. We lived there for a year and moved back onto the territory when I was in the fifth grade.

So basically, other than those few years, I've spent my life here at Onondaga.

The other day my son Neal and I were sitting there and we were talking about the things that we did when we were kids, growing up here on the rez. And where we played. And he said, "Gee, what about the kids downtown? Where do they play?"

So we got in the car and we drove into Nedrow and then down Salina Street and right into the city of Syracuse. And as we drove through the city, on various corners we would find kids standing around on the sidewalk, talking, but not playing or anything, you know.

And so I said, "What a shame." I said, "There's not even a tree in sight." They're standing on the corner, on the sidewalk: no grass, no trees, no animals. Just buildings and roads, cars. And what a difference between their place and the rez.

If you happen to be traveling down Route 81 South from Syracuse to Lafayette, you come to a big sign that says "Onondaga Nation Territory." And you pass that sign, you go around a slight turn, and then you head down a straightaway. And during the straightaway, there's a bridge across

Route 81 that you go under. That's Sentinel Heights Road. And from there, if you look straight ahead down Route 81, you will see a big hill. That was my backyard. And it was Neal's front yard.

Right now, the house that I live in is across the road from the house where I spent my first years as a boy. My father's parents' house is right across the road from where I live today. There is a creek that runs right alongside of our yard—our yard where we used to mow the lawn. We'd mow right up to the creek.

And that creek empties into Onondaga Creek. And it's called . . . it has two names: Hemlock Creek and Little Creek. Onondaga Creek was Big Creek. So Hemlock Creek was Little Creek.

But growing up on the rez, it would take you forty-five minutes to get from where I lived to the top of that big hill. And once you reached the top, I think it was a mile wide and two miles long on top of the hill. So my backyard was big. It consisted of about 3,000 acres of land, full of animals—deer, muskrats, chipmunks, squirrels, owls, bunny rabbits. This is where I hunted, and this is where I played.

And Neal tells about him and his buddy—Boots, Boy Boots—coming down that hill in the wintertime, sliding. And he tells about the times that he spent up in the woods on this same hill that I played on as a child.

But what a difference between my backyard and his front yard, and the yards of the children in the city! There's no comparison between the two.

Now my cousin, Oren Lyons, says that he learned more about life on that hill than he did going to school in the city and having them teach him about how life is. He learned more in the woods from the animals than he did from the books and the academics of the school system.

And learning from the animals is a big part of our life. For instance, it seems to me that most of the white community have not learned to live like the animals. If you go into the woods, as I mentioned before, there are rabbits, chipmunks, squirrels, raccoons, deer, turkeys. . . . And each one of them has their own identity as to who they are. They have their own territory and they all live together in peace, in harmony with each other, respecting each other for their differences.

And the wolf is not trying to change the coyote to be a wolf. The wolf respects the coyote for being a coyote, for being what he is. He doesn't say, "My life is better, you should live like me and you should be like me." Whereas, what happened to us is we had Europeans come into our country saying that their way of life was better than ours. So they attempted to change us to be like them.

And some of our people did change, but there are many of them who did not change. And we still remain who we were, remain who we are. We're Onondaga, citizens of the Haudenosaunee. And as such we have responsibilities and mandates as citizens of the Onondaga and the Haudenosaunee, to maintain and preserve our way of life.

Those that were changed by the white society don't know these things. They weren't taught that.

So that was my front yard. My side yard and my backyard were the same, woods and streams. Really my yard consisted of 7,300 acres of land. There were five streams of water, which had trout and whitefish and bass in them. And so I fished all of my years as a teenager, and growing up, so that we would have something to eat for supper, or for dinner. And Oren did the same thing. And we learned from our fathers to respect the animals in the forest. We learned that we were in their homes and that we should not disrupt or disturb their homes. If we went through, we were to make sure that we didn't disturb them.

And because we grew up this way, today we teach our children the same things. And all of the stories that my father told me as I was growing up, I use in today's lectures. I use them when I talk about the environment and the preservation of what's here today for tomorrow and future generations. And I use them when I talk about the violations of our treaties, which have created a situation we now know as global warming.

My father would tell me what he used to see when he was young. And then when I grew up and I was in the woods and in the streams, I never saw what he saw. So the outside people who surrounded us were changing the world. They changed it so that I did not see the same things that my father saw. That's why I'm able to talk about the environment, and working with the community—meaning the environment—for preservation.

So that our grandchildren will be able to enjoy the same things that we enjoy today: clean air, clean water, fish, animals in the woods, and so forth. So that we can learn from them.

As I said, most people have not learned to live like the animals in the woods. We have also not learned to live like the animals in the barnyard. We have cows, horses, pigs, goats, chickens, ducks, and so forth, all living together in peace and harmony. There's no fighting among those animals. They don't try to change another to be like themselves. There's no fighting over territory, not like in today's world where there are always fights over territories.

We, as supposedly the most intelligent of the animals—because we have a brain—have not learned to live in peace with each other. Humans have not learned to live like the animals, in peace and harmony with each other. There are wars. There's been a constant war going on for the last 40,000 years. So we have a lot to learn from the animals. And if we learned from the animals, there would be no wars in this world. Because most of all we would have respect for each other. And we do not seem to have that.

So this was the big difference between growing up on the rez and growing up in the city. In the city, people don't have the same opportunities to learn these things. They don't learn about the environment and their relationship to a tree or to a plant or to the animals. There's a lack of respect for them, probably because they're not part of that. And Western civilization does not recognize the life of the trees, the plants, the hills, the stones, the mountains. These *all* have lives. They're all alive, as far as we're concerned.

Some people have learned about—you might question the word—the "life" of a stone. Stones are alive. They have a life. They're full of minerals they've accumulated over the years. And today, if you find a place that does it, you can go to a store and buy stone dust. And you can use stone dust as a fertilizer. Because the stone dust is right next to being turned back into earth. And it contains minerals. It contains all kinds of life. And so when you put it in your garden, the life of the stone then gets transferred into Mother Earth and becomes part of the plant. And so the plant grows healthy, strong, full of minerals. It's much better for you than the ones that you put insecticides on—insecticides, which are not good for you.

But growing up on the reservation I learned stuff that's different from what most people learn growing up in the city. It's a big difference, especially when you look at my front yard, that big hill. And that's what they call it in Onondaga, "the big hill."

My dad would tell me, "There were so many fish in that stream of water that it looked like you could walk across the stream on the backs of the fish, because the fish were from bank to bank." I have never seen anything like that. I have seen a lot of fish in the water, but never that many, where they went from bank to bank But from my dad's life to my life, changes have come about, so that that situation no longer exists. You don't find streams that have that many fish in them. And from my life to your life there are even less fish.

In fact, many of the fish that used to be around when he was a child are not around now, today. Onondaga Lake used to have sturgeons. There are no sturgeons in there now. And I don't know about the whitefish, but I spent my whole teenage years fishing Onondaga Creek, catching whitefish. And I would bring them home and we would have that for dinner.

And it wasn't until much later that I found out that we were actually having a real delicacy. Because whitefish was a fish that was cooked in the various restaurants around here, fish they caught in Onondaga Lake or in the creek. It was such a beautiful fish to eat that people came from miles around to eat the whitefish out of our creek. And I don't know whether they're still in Onondaga Lake or not. And I don't know about the creek, because I haven't fished in years.

I don't fish now because I'm in a wheelchair and I can't walk along the creeks. And I don't know whether Oren still fishes or not, but he and I spent a lot of time fishing. And we spent a lot of time with my father fishing at the various lakes and the creeks. My father used to go up. . . .

We have a dam on our territory, that was built in the 1940s by the Army Corps of Engineers. They figured that if they put a dam up there, they would save Syracuse from being flooded every spring. Well, we told them that wouldn't do it. But they built the dam anyway and it didn't stop the flooding.

My father used to go up there, opposite the dam, and where the water came through the dam it ended up in a pool. So the water came rushing through a little faster than usual, because it was coming through a tunnel, and then it came into this pool. So this was a place where trout would sit and wait for food.

So my father used to go up there and throw his bait into the creek and let it float into the pool. And it would catch trout. And because Oren and I spent so much time with my father doing this stuff, he would tell us stories while we were fishing. And my father said, in the environment, "Take only what you need, when you need it, and whatever you take, use."

So when I went hunting, I shot one pheasant, or one rabbit, and came home. Because after I shot one, I was through hunting.

Oren's and my time, spent in the woods with the animals, enabled us now to travel around the world, speaking about conservation of the animals, the fish, the plants, and the trees. He has traveled all over the world. He's been to Russia; he's been to the UN; he's been to Oxford, England, teaching what he learned as a child on the rez.

And when I go out, this is what I do: I tell stories that my dad told me. And I use them as stories about why we need to preserve. Because if we don't, our grandchildren will not be able to enjoy what we enjoy today. There will be no rabbits. And we know this to be a fact. The Europeans came into our territory in 1788. Before that, the homing pigeons that traveled from north to south every spring and fall used to darken the sky, there were so many. And today there are only two. And they are stuffed and they're in museums—one in Rochester and one in a Seneca museum. All the rest have been extinguished. There are none.

And if people continue to do like they're doing, they're going to eliminate the animal world. And they'll fish every day until there are no more fish. They go out and they destroy forests. They get their big machinery and they clear-cut everything.

But a tree has a life, and it has a purpose. And its purpose is to give oxygen to us. And if you eliminate the trees, you are eliminating something that we need. That's why there's a big push to preserve the forest in South America along the Amazon River. Because of the oxygen that comes out of that forest.

And we, the Native people anyway, have learned how to live with the environment and preserve it, so that it'll be here tomorrow. We have told over and over again to the people that we have met—starting in the early 1600s, when people from the Netherlands came into our territory and wanted to live with us—we said, "You can live with us as long as you live by the natural laws."

And after that we made treaties with Great Britain, and the United States, always in peace and friendship. That was the main thing. We said that we would live together. We would coexist under natural laws, preserving what's here today for tomorrow. And the last time that I heard a reference to this was in 1794 at Canandaigua when Timothy Pickering, representing the United States, said that he was negotiating, "so that the chain of friendship would be brightened." Which means that we will live in peace and harmony with each other and the environment. But no one says that now. And I think that message that we gave back in the early 1600s got lost somehow.

But I thought I would give this little insight as to the difference between living in a city and living in the Indian community, where you learn about life and the preservation of life, so that you will be able to survive years from now.

We will survive, if we're left like we are.

But the Western civilization, if their people continue to pollute and destroy, they're going to destroy what's here today. And there will be nothing here for tomorrow. A very important lesson.

So I spent a lot of time along the banks of these five streams—South Hollow, Onondaga Creek, Hemlock Creek, Williams Creek, and Jake Springs—obtaining fish for dinner. They were all full of fish. And so we're used to having trout for dinner. And some of these trout that we obtained were twenty-three inches long. My cousin Oren and I went down to Williams Creek one day and we took three fish: twenty-one, twenty-two, and twenty-three inches. He took the twenty-two inch one; I took the twenty-one inch one. The twenty-three inch one, we cut in half lengthwise. And we each took one half of it.

So now his family had dinner and my family had dinner. That's the way Oren and I grew up. We grew up in the woods and along the banks of these five streams. And this is where we learned about life, in the woods, with nature, and along the streams. And listening to the stories our fathers told us about who we were: Native people with the job of preserving the environment for tomorrow and future generations.

As I went through that, my dad said to me, "I want you to graduate from high school." So I was going to Onondaga Valley Academy, which is a high school in the Valley—a section of Syracuse called "the Valley." I graduated from there in 1947.

And I didn't intend to go to college. So I just bummed around for a few years. And then the Korean War broke out. And Oren, his brother, my brothers, and I went into the Korean War. And we came out in 1954.

In 1955 I was married. I got married and we lived here at Onondaga. And I was married to Helen for forty-six years.

During this time, because of my knowledge of the Onondagas and their history and the environmental issues and so forth, and because of my fights with the state on jurisdiction, sovereignty, and so forth, I was asked to attend colleges and make presentations.

So for almost fifty years this is what I did. And because of the work that I did with the state on sales tax, and because of the work that I did with the government on the issues on sovereignty and so forth, I became pretty well known, and I was frequently requested to present at the universities.

I've spoken at Cornell, Colgate, Hobart, Syracuse, Buffalo Law College, and Stanford University in California. I spent four days down at Stanford with all the law students, explaining Indian law. And at Buffalo I presented the conflict between federal Indian law, state Indian law, and the *real* Indian law: Onondaga and Haudenosaunee law.

So I was asked to make presentations about the stories that I told. And as I went through learning not only about my history, I also learned about the history between our people, the state of New York, and the United States. And I learned about the relationships and the events that happened throughout history when our leaders met with the incoming people from Europe.

In 1945, I met my first "expert." I was walking along Route 11A, which goes right through the center of our territory. And I was in front of the school. A car stopped. And this young man got out of the car—suit, white shirt, and tie—and informed me that he was a professor at a university in Arizona, an expert on Indians. And he would like to know where the Indian village was.

So I looked at him. I said to myself, *This man is an expert on Indians? And he wants to know where the Indians are? And he's looking for tipis in Haudenosaunee territory?* I said, *This guy doesn't know anything about the Haudenosaunee and he's not an expert.*

So I directed him to a path, a road that headed east. I said, "Go up that road. At the end of the road you'll find a path. The path will take you up on top of that hill over there. That's where the village is." I said, "You probably won't find any men there, because they're already hunting, getting ready for the winter."

So he said, "Thank you." And he left. And I went down the street laughing, knowing full well that there was nobody up there. There was no village. In fact, we weren't hunting and getting ready for the winter.

It wasn't 'til years later that I happened to be talking to the principal of the school about different things that had happened to her while she was principal. And she told me, she said, "You know, one day, I was sitting in my office and this man walked in, and he said, 'I spent the whole day up on top of that hill looking for the Indian village,' he said. 'And I never did find it.'"

She said, "You didn't?"

He said, "Some young man told me out there that I could find an Indian village up on top of the hill. And I've been all over that hill all day long," he said. "And I've been unable to find it."

And she laughed. And when she told me about it, I said, "I sent that man up on top of that hill."

She said, "You did?"

I said, "Yeah." So we had a good chuckle over that.

Anyway, she had graduated from college. And out of college, she came straight to Onondaga. There was a teacher's job open and she came into our school when she was about seventeen years old. And she retired from our school, from teaching. So she was there for years.

And she started way in the kindergarten. There was a time when she was at the school that she had taught everybody who lived here, that had gone through the school system. Most of them, you know, reluctantly, had gone to school. And if they went to school, they went to kindergarten. And she taught them there. And then she taught other grades. So over the years, she'd taught everybody on the territory.

And she was really surprised one day when she went down to the playground. And we were playing ball at recess. And she said, "Who's winning? What's the score?"

And we said, "We're not keeping score. And we don't know who's winning."

She said, "Well then, why are you playing?"

We said, "We're playing because we enjoy playing the game. It doesn't matter who wins or who loses. The idea is to play the game and enjoy it and have fun."

And she said, "That concept is not in my society. And these Native people, these kids are playing for the fun of the game, not to see who wins or loses, but just to say that they played. It's one of their Native sports."

So she talked about who we were, what kind of people we were. She carried that thought throughout her whole time she was here at Onondaga, that we were different-thinking, had a different perspective on life. She really cherished the time. And every time she went out, she mentioned the different concept of sportsmanship between the outside world and what's at Onondaga. And she really hated to retire, but she finally had to. She was getting up there in age where she couldn't really take it anymore, the full job of teaching. So she retired.

Anyway, life here at Onondaga is different than the outside world. And I wasn't really aware of that until I went into the outside world. When I went to school at Onondaga Valley, I was the only male Indian in the school. And a lot of those kids had never seen an Indian before. And of course they had the image and the history of us through movies. So they expected me to have feathers in my hair, growing out of my head. They expected me to be like what they'd seen in the movies.

And since I wasn't, they really didn't understand that. And then because of the movies and what was portrayed in them, some of them did not like Indians. So I was in a lot of fights. But because I was in the woods and along the creeks and doing things in the manner of our elders, I was lean and strong. Not very big, but muscular, a lot of strength because of my lifestyle. Whereas they were in the city where there were no trees. There was no place for them to go and do things like me and Oren.

So I didn't lose any fights while I was there, in the six years I was there. Then I graduated from there, went in the navy. Also had fights in the navy. But I learned, you know, as I was growing up, the difference between their world and my world. And this is what I present in most of my lectures, this concept of a different perspective of life, which really amazed the kids I was talking to, the college kids

Who are these people anyway?

Anyway, through this whole process, of meeting this first white guy way back in 1945, the question came up in my mind, *Who are these people anyway?*

And one day when I was in my house, I was looking at the books that I have. And there was a book on white and Indian relationships. And I opened up the book, leafed through it, and I stopped on a page. There were notes by a historian that told about the Natives meeting the people from across the waters, in Albany.

And the Natives watched these people from across the waters take from their back pockets pieces of white cloth. And they discharged the contents of their noses into these cloths. Then they carefully folded up each white cloth into a square and saved the contents of their noses. They stuck them back in their back pockets. And my people said to themselves, *Who are these people anyway?*

So I said, "Wow, that's very interesting, that even my ancestors were asking the same question, 'Who are these people anyway?'"

Recently, on the Jay Leno show, Leno mentioned that a celebrity was at his program and was being interviewed. The celebrity had to use a facial tissue, to take care of their nose. And so the following week, Leno took that facial tissue, and he put it on eBay, for sale. And he sold it for $4,272. Who are these people anyway? Not only do they save it, but they'll also *buy* it!

So anyway, as I went along, I kept meeting these "experts" who were totally unaware of who we were. So it brought the question up, which I thought I would make the title of my book, *Who Are These People Anyway?*

And I started making mental notes on these people and what they do. For instance, I understand that many non-Native people see better standing up than they do sitting down. Now, for an example, they go to a football game. And they've all got seats. And sitting in these seats they can see the entire field, from goal line to goal line. And the quarterback goes back and he throws a pass to a receiver. And the receiver runs down the sidelines toward the goal line. Now before he crosses the goal line and makes a touchdown, guess what happens? Everybody stands up, so they can see better, I guess. I don't know. That's what I think, anyway. And I'm going, *Who are these people anyway, that see better standing up than they do sitting down?*

Anyway, that's just one example. There are many things that a lot of non-Native people do that we don't understand. And so we ask the question, "Who are these people anyway?"

I don't suppose I'm going to be able to cover all of the various instances I've noticed. So when I finish, you can continue with the things that you know that you do that would make our people ask the question, "Who are these people anyway?" Because of the differences.

There are treaty obligations on both sides

Well, a lot of things are happening, not just right here in Onondaga, but internationally. So I thought I would tell you about international treaties and the Sherrill Decision, the 2005 US Supreme Court decision regarding the Oneida Nation. This is important because most people don't know about the treaties. The treaties are important. It's important to understand that the treaties were made not only by us, but by the United States, for the protection of us and into the future. And those of you who are citizens of the United States, if you don't know about the treaties, you don't know that you're the other half of the treaties.

And at Onondaga and all of the other Haudenosaunee nations, we all know that we have treaties and there are treaty obligations on both sides. We have treaty obligations to you; you have obligations to us. So it's important, because I know you don't teach this in the school system. You don't teach too much about us. I talk to college graduates: they know nothing about the Haudenosaunee.

I lectured at Utica one day to 250 prospective state troopers. And I said, "I'm probably going to tell you about history that you don't know about, so how many people know about the Haudenosaunee?"

Not one hand went up.

I was talking to people who'd never heard about us, so it was tough to explain to them the position of a sovereign nation within the state of New York. And they didn't understand it. But this is what this is about.

So I'm going to start with the first international treaty. This was made in the early 1600s. We remember it through a wampum belt, the Two Row, between the people from the Netherlands and the Haudenosaunee.

And I've been talking about this agreement for many years. It's a very important treaty because it establishes how we will coexist here on Mother Earth.

We will know each other as brothers

Back then we had people coming into our territory and we didn't know who they were. And so we went up to talk with them.

And I was thinking about this the other day. And I said, "I don't understand . . . I don't really understand how this happened, but you have people from the Netherlands coming here who don't speak Onondaga. And the Onondagas don't speak Dutch. But these two people got together, and they were able to communicate back and forth. And that dialogue that went back and forth was then told over and over again. From generation to generation it came down so that my father told me about it."

He said, "This is what happened. This is what they said."

And I said, "Well, that's interesting." Here we are in the year 2007 and we all speak English and we have problems communicating, because we don't understand each other. But how was it that in the early 1600s two peoples from different languages were able to sit down and communicate back and forth? Well, remember that the Dutch had been trading in the Hudson River Valley since 1598, and I guess each side had time to learn some of the basics in each other's language.

So what came down to us was that these people wanted to come into our lands and establish a trade agreement and to purchase lands from us. And so we sat there. . . . Now, at this time, it's undetermined how long we sat there to make this agreement. But it was agreed upon, finally.

But during discussion, the Dutch people said, "Well, in the future, when we meet, we think it would be a good idea if you called us 'father' and we would call you 'son.'"

So we thought about this a while, about father and son relationships. And we said, "No, that's not a good idea. We will discuss and greet each other as brothers."

So the Dutch said, "All right."

They bump hips

Now to show you another difference between our people and yours, let's go back to what I was saying about how we play our games for our enjoyment. And let's talk a little about lacrosse. Today we're going to talk about *dehoñtshihgwaʔes* (day-hoon-tshih-GWA-es), which means "they bump hips." This is a game that the Creator gave to us years ago for his entertainment. So when we play this game, we are entertaining him.

And the game is made up of his rules and regulations so that we learn how to work together as a team, to make split-second decisions on what is happening. And it gives us a chance to display our gifts that the Creator has given us, like the ability to run and to handle a stick. This game is known by us as dehoñtshihgwaʔes but, over the years, because of the French and the Europeans coming into our country and watching us play, they now call the game lacrosse.

Lacrosse at Onondaga is considered sacred. It is a game to be played for the Creator, and has been known to have healing power. The game in its original form is played between two groups, usually either divided up by clans or by age (young men versus old men). Since women are respected for providing life and are to protect this gift, they do not play lacrosse.

Once sides are chosen, the two teams play. The men hold in their hands hand-made sticks, usually made of hickory. The spirit of the tree connects the player to Mother Earth while they play for the Creator. The game is played on an open field with two poles at each end, signifying goals, which a ball made of leather must pass through.

As our white brothers began to play, the growth of our game allowed our people to play lacrosse in many different arenas. Soon the Onondagas were playing field lacrosse with the local colleges and universities in the area. It was very common for Onondaga to play Syracuse University, Colgate University, and the army in the early 1900s.

Then in 1932, the Olympics wanted to showcase lacrosse in the upcoming games in Los Angeles. The Onondaga Nation team was very polished and was undefeated in the area. A playoff was established and it was a match between the Onondagas and a team from Johns Hopkins, to play each other to represent the games at the Olympics. Johns Hopkins prevailed, but both teams respected each other's play. These days, it's played by high schools, colleges, and professional teams throughout the world.

I was five years old when I received my first stick, made out of hickory with a rawhide netting on which to catch and carry the ball. My father gave it to me. And then we went out into the front yard and we played catch with a rubber ball. Old lacrosse was played with a ball made out of leather. And the type that my father and I were playing with is made out of India rubber. It's hard; it bounces very well off the fields. And later, when we played box lacrosse, it bounced well off the wooden floors and concrete floors that we played on.

So anyway, at the age of five I received my first stick. At the age of nine I received my second stick, which was made out of white ash. And I have played in the old way, in a field with two sticks stuck in the ground as the goal. And I wore no pads. The stick that I got in 1939 lasted me until 1949. Ten years, I played with it.

That stick lasted me until I was nineteen years old. When I was seventeen and eighteen, I played field lacrosse against the colleges around the area like Hobart, Cortland, Colgate, Cornell, and Syracuse University. So by the time I was nineteen years old, I had been playing on the men's team for two years.

And my next stick lasted me until 1971. And other people who played, when I wasn't playing, would come and borrow my stick, because it was so good. It was a very light stick and very accurate. You could put the ball where you wanted to, with it. So lacrosse players would come to my house and borrow my stick. I said, "Well, you can borrow it, but don't break it." And fortunately for me they kept coming back. But after years of use that stick finally wore out and I had to get a new one. So in 1971 I bought a new stick, which I still have.

Unfortunately, with the success of the Onondaga team against the collegiate teams, the national association, US Lacrosse, banned all Native teams from playing field lacrosse because they felt that the Natives were "professional" players.

Since the Onondagas and the rest of the Haudenosaunee couldn't play field lacrosse, they turned their attention northward where the Canadians were starting a new kind of lacrosse. The Canadians began playing lacrosse inside empty hockey rinks. The Onondagas and the Haudenosaunee quickly took to the physical nature of the game where intricate stick skills were fostered in "box lacrosse." Soon box lacrosse leagues became commonplace in the communities of the Haudenosaunee. From that point on, players became so adept at the box game that players such as Lyle Pierce and Stanley Pierce, and my father, Irving Powless Sr., were inducted into the National Lacrosse Hall of Fame [Class of 2000] for their prowess on the field.

So by the time I was nineteen, we had formed a box lacrosse league. And from 1949 to 1971, a period of twenty-two years, I played box lacrosse.

Field and box lacrosse are totally different games. When the Europeans started playing the game, well, we played on an open field with two sticks stuck into the ground as goal posts. And the ball had to go between the two posts. And we had limits on how many scores would be made before one would be declared the winner so that the games didn't last forever. If you made three goals, you were the winner. Therefore the game was not timed.

And when the Europeans started playing the game, they changed the game completely. In the old way, everybody who showed up at our games was able to play. I've played in games where we had teenagers and eighty-year-old men playing on the same team, with an unlimited number of players on each team. We had the goalposts but there were no sidelines, so you could run anywhere. And you could run anywhere between the goalposts.

But the Europeans changed the rules. They put in a centerline and they put limits on the numbers. They put ten players on a field lacrosse team and five players on a box lacrosse team. In box lacrosse half the team only played on one half of the court. And field lacrosse was the same way. So it restricted the play.

I played box lacrosse for twenty-two years and for twenty-one of those years I played without a helmet. And in the twenty-second year, we started playing against Europeans who had different rules, regulations, and methods of play. The way we play, we play with no pads, no helmet, no face guards, no gloves, and we play only with wooden sticks. With the invention of plastic, today you have plastic sticks and big rule changes. So when I started playing box lacrosse against the Europeans, I had to wear a helmet to protect myself.

But we played to entertain the Creator, so nobody got hurt. We tried to hit the sticks, to knock the ball out of the stick. And we bumped hips to knock the opponent down, so he would not be able to score. That's why the game is called "they bump hips."

This bumping of hips is a technique all by itself. My dad started playing when he was fifteen years old. He was playing field lacrosse. Later he played professional lacrosse, box lacrosse, for Syracuse and Rochester. And when I was learning to play he said, "When we played, we bumped hips and this is how we did it."

And so I listened to him very carefully and I said, "I'm going to try this out." So one day when we were playing, a guy came running by. I watched, and the words of my father came into my head. And I watched this man coming at me, and I watched his feet. Now the timing has to be just right, in order to do this. So when the timing was right, I moved and I bumped his hip.

And down he went.

And I said, "Wow, it really works!" And so I kept doing this, and the more I did it, the better I got at it. After not too long, I was pretty proficient at it. And I became known as this kind of a player, that would bump into you and knock you down. And I knocked down a lot of people.

Playing field lacrosse, I came up against All-Americans who had never played in a game where the old way was played. And these All-Americans were six foot and they weighed 200 pounds. I was a strapping 144 pounds. But by playing for twenty-two years, I was strong. And so when these big guys came running at me, I had no fear about bumping into them. And of course they didn't expect to be bumped, so when they got knocked down, they were really surprised.

One of the persons that I knocked down was named Bill Fuller, three-time All-American center for Syracuse [University] (SU) and the leading high scorer on the team. At halftime he was scoreless. I had knocked him down three times as he tried to make it in toward the net to score a goal. And Roy Simmons Sr., their lacrosse coach, was really mad at what I was doing. So he instructed his team to get me. He said, "I want that man taken out."

And now I'm up there, I've got ten players trying to nail me. And they finally got their chance. I was standing near the center line and I hollered for a pass. Howie Hill threw me one of those looping passes, and it stayed up in the air for a while. So the defensemen could see where the ball was going. And I was just standing there.

The two defensemen came rushing at me. As one hit me from the front, the other one hit me from the back. Fortunately for me, they met me at the same time. So they canceled out the checks. There was a loud crash as the three of us banged into each other. And, of course, all three of us went down.

But I wasn't hurt. If I had just been hit by one of them, I would've gone flying one way. But because I got hit the same time from front and back, I didn't go anywhere. The referee came over and he blew his whistle. And he penalized both defensemen for unnecessary roughness. He gave them each a minute penalty.

And then I stood up. And he said, "Are you all right?"

And I said, "Yeah, I'm all right." I said, "Give me the ball."

He said, "What?"

I said, "Give me the ball, so we can continue playing."

He said, "After that hit, you're going to play?"

I said, "Well yeah, I'm all right." I said, "It's only a body check. So I'm used to that. Give me the ball."

So he put the ball in my stick and blew the whistle. I was playing midfield. But I threw the ball over to Ed Shenandoah, another midi, and then I went for the goal. And I hollered for a pass. He passed the ball back to me and I took a couple of steps and wound up. And I shot for the net and I scored a goal.

This, of course, infuriated the SU coach, Roy Simmons. "I told you to get that guy. He's knocking down our players and now he's scoring on us." And I just laughed. And we went off the field and faced off again. And we played.

So for the rest of the game I had the whole team chasing me. We lost the game because we didn't have any substitutes and they had probably about forty or fifty players out there. So they just ran us to the ground. But we had fun. We enjoyed ourselves and it didn't matter that we lost. It was the idea that we had played. We had entertained the Creator by playing his game.

That's what we were supposed to do. And that's what we did.

And when we played box lacrosse, I was doing the same thing. I used the same technique to knock down the big guys in box lacrosse.

And then I went into the service. And I was in the Korean War. When the Korean War ended, I was over in the Mediterranean. And they immediately sent us back to the United States. So we got back to Norfolk, and they discharged me there, in August of 1954. I came back home and I got engaged to be married, very quickly, like in December of '54. And I was married in March of '55. And in 1955 I was back to playing box lacrosse again.

One day we invited the Mohawks down to play with us. And at the last moment they called up and said, "We're not coming." And so we asked Syracuse University to bring their team down to play. They said, "Field lacrosse?"

We said, "No, we play box lacrosse."

They said, "All right, we'll try it out."

So this was 1957. And by this time I had put on weight. I weighed 155 pounds. I had gained over ten pounds since I was playing earlier at 144 pounds. But I still had all the moves and all the knowledge. And so our team was out there playing. And the ball went into the corner and they blew the whistle, which gave us time to change strings. Our string came out, so I went out on the court with them.

At the same time that I went out on the court, Syracuse changed their string. And Jim Brown, the famous football player, ran out on the field.

And there was a big fight for the ball over in the east corner of the box. Well, he went into that fight for the ball, scooped up the ball, and came out with the ball and headed west toward his goal, the goal he was supposed to score in.

As he started downfield, I was the only one standing between him and the goal. And he took one look at me and he said to himself, *Well, I'll go right by this guy.* So he came pounding by at top speed, at 235 pounds. And as he went by me, I bumped his hip. And down he went: it was the first time he had ever been knocked down in a lacrosse game, *any* lacrosse game. He played high school, he played college, and he'd never been knocked down. He was in our box lacrosse game thirty seconds and he was lying on his back. I guess he found it unbelievable.

After the game, I got a chance to meet him. Oren Lyons was on the same team as he was. And Jim Brown said to Oren, he said, "Introduce me to that mosquito that knocked me down."

So Oren brought him over to me. And I only came up to his chest. I had a twenty-four inch waist. Jim Brown had twenty-four inch thighs! But the technique that I had learned from my father enabled me to bump hips against Jim Brown. And down he went.

This was quite an event, because I know for about ten years after that game, they were still talking about it when lacrosse players got together down in the Syracuse area.

But here's something that was more surprising. Just last year, the Iroquois' national lacrosse team was going to go over to England to play in the world games. And the United States and England decided that they would not accept our passports. They said, in order for us to go to England, we had to have either US or Canadian passports.

And we said, "No, there's no way that we're going to go over there as citizens of another country. We're coming over as Haudenosaunee with our own passports, or we're not coming."

They said, "Well, you can't come over unless you've got a US passport or a Canadian."

We said, "Well, we're not coming." And we didn't go.

So *Sports Illustrated* put an article in their magazine about that incident where we were denied going to play in the world games over in

England. But in the article, down at the bottom of one of the pages, it says, "At a game in 1957, an Onondaga who later became one of the chiefs of the Onondaga Nation, who weighed 155 pounds, ran up against Jim Brown, who weighed 235 pounds, and knocked him down."

Now this is fifty-seven years after the incident, and it's still being news! And here it was in *Sports Illustrated*, which is quite a thing for me, you know, to be still talked about, after all of those years. Fifty-seven years later, we're still talking about that.

I played from the time I was seventeen until I was forty-one. And during that time, I have no idea how many goals I scored. I don't know how many games I played in. We never kept track of this stuff. We just played and had fun.

And now the Onondagas excel in both the field and the box game. For example, Oren Lyons (Syracuse University All-American goaltender) is in the National Lacrosse Hall of Fame. He and Travis Cook, Russ George, Eli Cornelius, Louis Jacques, and my son Barry have been recognized on both sides of the border in various halls of fame. Current stars of both the professional field and box games are Marshall Abrams (SU All-American), Gewas Schindler (Loyola All-American), and another one of my sons, Neal Powless (Nazareth All-American). And there are many more great players on the horizon.

Unfortunately, today, the colleges that play lacrosse don't play with the same connection with the Creator. So they play lacrosse totally different than how it's supposed to be played. And so the game has changed a whole lot since the time when my grandfather and my father played, and since the games that I played at Onondaga, where we played only with wooden sticks. We didn't allow the newly made plastic sticks in the game. And we played according to our old rules. We didn't wear gloves; we didn't wear any pads; we didn't wear helmets or face guards. And nobody got hurt during those games.

The way they play now, it's dangerous to get into one of those games. Because they use their sticks, the plastic sticks, to supposedly hit the stick of the opponent. But they miss a lot of times and they hit the player. Therefore the player has got rib pads on, he's got shoulder pads on, and he's got arm pads on to protect himself. And a helmet and a face guard.

I never had those things. I played box lacrosse for twenty-one years without a helmet. I never put a helmet on until the last year I played, when I was forty-one years old. And that year I got hit in a body check in Fort Erie, Canada, on a concrete floor. When I landed on my shoulders, my head snapped back and I could hear my helmet click on the concrete. And I said, "Oh, I can see why I've got to wear a helmet," I said, "because if I didn't, I'd have a headache right now." I don't know how big a bump I would've gotten. But I did hear that click when my helmet hit the concrete floor.

And so I taught my boys the same, to play the game that way. One weekend my son Brad played up north with the Mohawks. When he came back, he brought his helmet back with him. And he showed his mother his helmet. And the helmet was smashed. And he said, "This is what the Mohawks did to me." He said, "I was running along the boards and they came up and they cross-checked me, and," he said, "they cross-checked me in the head. And they put my head up against the boards and smashed my helmet."

"And how about you?"

"Oh," he said, "I'm all right. My helmet got smashed, that's all."

So nothing much stopped them in those days. And they became All-Americans. They have records that still stand in college and in high school to this day. One of them is from 1975. Another one is from 1995. Their records are still standing.

Anyway, it's not necessary to know who's winning or who's losing. It's to play the game to enjoy the game, because you're entertaining the Creator. And that's the difference in the games, totally different games, between what we played and what they're playing now.

So when we play lacrosse here on Mother Earth, there's a game going on in the Creator's territory at the same time. And the ones who play lacrosse here, in the afterlife they're going to go there and continue to play.

Now we know this to be true because, in the 1800s, our ancestor, a Seneca leader named Handsome Lake, was given a message by his three Messengers from the Creator's land. These Messengers, they took him to the Creator's land. And while he was there, he watched a lacrosse game and he played lacrosse himself. And he watched a ceremony being conducted and he watched singers who were singing songs to the Creator, songs that were given to us by the Creator.

And then he came back home. And when he was back on Mother Earth, he was explaining to everybody what he had seen. He was telling them that the lacrosse players today will be able to play in the future up in the Creator's land, after they've passed away.

And one of the fellows that he was telling is one of the fellows that he had seen playing lacrosse up in the Creator's land. He happened to be talking to a man who he had seen in that other land. So he stopped talking, realizing, you know, that he was telling this man that he was going to pass away. So he was talking to this guy. And three days later, the man did pass away. And Handsome Lake said, "Well, I know where he is. He's playing lacrosse up in the Creator's land." So today we get buried with our sticks.

We have ceremonies with our ancestors. And when we have these ceremonies, there are ribbons given out. The ribbons from each ceremony then go onto the lacrosse stick. And so when we play lacrosse, that ensures that the ancestors are playing with us, because of the ceremonies that we had. And this is when scores don't matter. You play to entertain the Creator and you play to enjoy the game.

So our sticks are decorated with ribbons from this ceremony that we do when we dance with our elders. In the morning ribbons are given out. So I take and I decorate my lacrosse stick with those, so that the dance that we've done with our ancestors is now part of my stick. And I'll use that stick to play with my ancestors in the future.

So lacrosse is a very important game here at Onondaga. I was still playing at the age of seventy-one, in 2001. And on the team that day there were teenagers. And I was not the oldest one who was playing. Sandy Buck was playing and he must've been around eighty-three or eighty-four years old. But we played the old way, with wooden sticks, with no pads, no helmet. And we had a really good time.

Dehoñtshihgwa'es is a game given to us by the Creator to entertain him and to show our gifts: our ability to run and make split-second decisions, our ability to handle a stick, to pass, catch, and so forth. But the Creator also gave it to us to teach us how to work together as a team, to put our minds together as one. So we play the game to entertain the Creator. And we play so that we can play tomorrow, if necessary. So nobody gets hurt. No one.

But since we're playing according to European rules and regulations, it's not happening anymore. And unfortunately our young people are not talking to the real old people. They're not around. So they can't explain to them how the games are supposed to be played.

And so the game is not played that way today. And they not only play lacrosse in ways that cause injuries, but they'll play other games that way. They play basketball, they play football, and if there's someone good on the team, they try to wipe him out. I was reading in today's paper that Brett Favre, quarterback for the Vikings, was taken out. He got carried off the field with a head injury. And he probably won't be able to play anymore this season. He's got two more games to play; he probably won't play them. So it ended his season.

Anyway, that's the game that is called, in our language, "they bump hips." But in the English language, as it's used today, it's called lacrosse. And it's been played here at Onondaga for thousands of years. I don't know when the game was given to us, but down through the years, it's come through.

So, I thought that maybe you would be interested in what used to be and what is today. There's a big difference between the two.

Haudenosaunee actually means "people of the longhouse"

Long ago the Onondagas, as well as the Senecas, Cayugas, Oneidas, and Mohawks, dwelled in large bark homes that held members of a clan. These longhouses reached as long as 200 feet. As a means of protection, communities built large fences, referred to as palisades, around them. The longhouse is also an important symbol of the identity of the five nations. The union of five nations can be seen as a longhouse stretching across present-day New York State. The word Haudenosaunee actually means "people of the longhouse."

So historically, we are the People of the Longhouse. And we lived with 150 to 250 people in a house, probably a clan. And run by the clan mother. And so all the women in there were related; they were of that clan. And the women owned the house; they owned the property and so forth. And so if a man got married, he went to the home of his wife and lived with her clan. And so the women had a lot of control during this time.

And for some reason or other, I could never figure out, by the time of the Revolutionary War, we're not in longhouses. We're in single houses. Somewhere back there we changed from longhouses to single houses. And I couldn't understand why.

And then one of the historians was talking to us one day. And he said that in the 1600s, smallpox came into our community. It was introduced in the 1500s in Florida. And not very long after that, because our people were trading all over, smallpox was here in Haudenosaunee territory because it was introduced to the Seminoles by the Spaniards in Florida. And it was really wiping us out. And because it was contagious, in order to combat smallpox, this historian felt that we moved out of the longhouse and moved into individual homes.

So instead of being in the communal "clan" longhouse, the people were now in extended nuclear family cabins. We were separated. So this changed our whole lifestyle.

In the 1600s, smallpox killed thousands of our people. They figure that somewhere around 1600 or so, we had 100,000 Haudenosaunee. In the middle 1600s there were only 11,000 of us. We lost 90,000 people in just a short time. And it was all from smallpox. So this was a big turmoil among us.

And we're not the only ones who had it. The Europeans had smallpox, too. If you take a look at some of the paintings of George Washington and others, they've got rouge on. A lot of these men wore makeup. And the makeup that they wore was to fill up the holes or the pox in their faces. Because smallpox leaves an indentation in your face, or wherever it is. And so they would fill up those things with facial cosmetics so that they would be smooth.

But our people were not immune to those diseases and so when smallpox hit us, it just *destroyed* us.

And in the cemetery next to the longhouse, there's a section over there that has our people there, those who passed away because they had contracted smallpox. And I don't know exactly where it is, but it's there. Our elders have talked about it. Ed Shenandoah used to run the cemetery. His son Alan runs it now, but he told me about the small place over there in the cemetery where our people, our Onondagas, are buried—the ones who had smallpox. So smallpox is a very deadly disease that took a lot of our people.

Now the cabins were quite a size difference from the longhouse. Instead of the long rectangular homes, we built two-room cabins. Maybe the home had a second story. Here families continued to rely on aunts and grandparents to help raise the children.

Today, Onondagas live in a wide assortment of homes. At Onondaga, people build log homes, two-story homes, ranch style houses, and mobile homes. The banks do not lend money to people building on Onondaga land because the land and the home cannot be used as security for the loan. The property cannot be taken if the loan is not repaid. Therefore, homes that are built belong to the homeowners since they have raised the capital to build them.

The "World" Series

The people in the United States have a World Series in their baseball games. And the only teams that are invited to play in the World Series are teams from the United States. The teams in one league play against each other and determine a winner. The teams in the other league have a series and determine a winner. And then the two winning teams play against each other to find out who is the champion of the World Series.

And I was thinking, *Who are these people, anyway, who think that the United States is the world?* The little leaguers, they have a World Series. And they invite teams from *all* of the different nations—Japan, England, Australia. . . . But when the men play, they only play teams from the United States. And they call it the World Series. They're the best team "in the world." And after they determine who the best team in the world is (or in the United States), that team goes over to Europe and gets beaten by some of the teams in Europe!

So if they're going to have a *World* Series, then they should *have* a World Series. And invite teams from all of the nations to play, rather than just teams from the United States. But anyway, when I heard about this World Series in baseball, consisting of only teams from the United States, I said, *Well, who are these people, anyway, that think the United States is the world?*

That's all we need

Growing up here at Onondaga, with limited funds, it was necessary for us to go out and get the gifts that the Creator had left for us, to carry on and to live. He sent us rabbits, pheasants, partridges, raccoons, deer, and bear for us to eat. So growing up, I would go hunting with my dad and he would shoot one pheasant. And he would say, "Well, that's all we need." So after he would shoot one, we would stop hunting. It wasn't necessary to get more because all we needed was one for a meal. So we would come home.

When I was sixteen, my father gave me a used gun that he had bought from a guy when I was two years old. So the gun is probably older than I am. I still have the gun. And it's all oiled. The inside, the barrel, is just as shiny as it was when it was made.

And my dad explained to me that these are the natural laws that we live by: *Hunt only when necessary. And whatever you shoot, eat. Don't waste anything.* So I was growing up with this kind of thought from when I was a young boy.

Fighting over objects?

My cousin was telling me that his wife went to a sale in New York City at Macy's. And the people arrived at this sale *hours* before the doors opened. So at eight o'clock when the doors did open, there was a stampede. And these people knocked down people and then ran over them. And they killed one person in the stampede. Now who are these people that stampede at sales?

Once they got inside the store, there were fist fights between the women who were there, over a scarf or an object that was lying on the counter. And they both reached for it and they grabbed it at the same time. Now they're trying to get that item for themselves. And they're both hanging onto it. So they decide the best way to find out who's going to buy that item—if they decide to buy it—is to fight over it. So there are fistfights during this sale between these people. And when I heard that I said, *Who are these people anyway who go to a sale and then kill people in a stampede or fight over objects that are up for sale?* Big question.

And you will take care of them and preserve them for future generations

Now by the treaty that we made in the early 1600s, these people who came into our territory agreed that they would live in our territory. And we would coexist. And we said, "Well, you can come in and live with us, but you have to live under our rules."

And they said "All right. And what are your rules?"

We said, "You must obey the natural laws. And you must abide by the mandates that we have as members of the Onondaga Nation or the Haudenosaunee. And that is to respect Mother Earth, the trees, the animals, the fish, the air, the waters, the plants, and the medicines. And you will take care of them and preserve them for future generations. Usually we mention the seventh generation. We think seven generations ahead.

So we used to have clean water here. We used to have a beautiful lake down here called Onondaga Lake. But because the people who moved into our territory violated this treaty, we now have one of the most polluted lakes in the country. Our fish are gone. The animals that used to be here are gone.

Since the European people moved into our territory in 1788, they have polluted the land. They've violated this treaty. They did not live by these agreements that we had made. And so I present to you now this treaty. You—as the other half of this treaty—will see what you can do about making sure that your grandchildren will be able to enjoy the same things that we enjoy today. And if the ones before us have polluted, we will try to restore it to what it used to be.

And that's why the Onondagas are working so hard to clean up Onondaga Lake. Because that's how it's supposed to be. When the Europeans came to settle in our territory in 1788, you could drink the waters around. And when I was a teenager and I was hunting in Onondaga, I had no problems carrying a cup with me. And any time I came across a stream, I was able to dip my cup into the water and take a drink. You can't do that today. You can't go to the lake and take a drink, now.

There are other people who have the same kind of thinking as this now. A couple of years ago some Mongolians came to our territory. They have a lake up there in their territory the same size as Lake Ontario. It's 130 miles long. It's ten miles wide. And today you can go up to that lake and dip a glass into that water and drink it. You can't do that with Lake Ontario. You can't eat the fish that come out of that lake because of the violation of the treaty that we made.

So anyway, this is an international treaty. This is a treaty made between the Dutch people and the Haudenosaunee. And we made other treaties after that.

Lurking?

I hunted with my dad from the time I was fifteen, in 1945, until he passed away in 1985. So I spent forty years in the woods with my dad. And all the time that we were together, he never taught me how to "lurk."

If you read the books, it says the Indians were "lurking" behind the trees. But he didn't know how to "lurk" and he never taught me how to "lurk." So I don't know how to lurk. But it's something that's in the books that we do these things. And I'm here to tell you that we don't do these things because we don't know what they mean by it.

And who are these people that write about this, in this manner, and make up stories and put them in the books? And then people believe that this is what we do. I spent forty years with my father in the woods and he never went behind a tree and said, "This is how you lurk."

Haudenosaunee humor 1

Anyway, we don't lurk. But it's in the books that this is what we do. Also in the books is that we are stoic or stony-faced people who have no humor.

But we have humor. We have a lot of funny things that happen in our lives. When you have a group of our people together, there is laughter *all* the time. There's always something funny being said. And most of it is humor that only *we* understand. It's just funny to us.

Now I don't know if this will be funny to you, but it was funny to me and my son when it happened. I was watching TV and Tina Turner was on. And she's sixty-one years old, and she's up there singing and dancing and shaking. And my son, who's in his forties now, was sitting there with me, watching her. And because he doesn't play lacrosse anymore, he says he's "over the hill."

So I said to him, "Brad," I said, "Look at that Tina Turner. Look, she's sixty-one years old. Look at her. She's up there and she's sixty-one and you're forty-one and you're saying you're over the hill?" I said, "Take another look at this."

And he said to me, "Yeah, but she's never been cross-checked."

And I burst out laughing, and I said, "Yeah and she never got her helmet squushed or smashed." And we were sitting there laughing, because this was funny to us. In a lacrosse game you get banged around quite a bit. So at forty-one you're not playing anymore. You're over the hill. But she's up there, she's never played lacrosse, and she never got cross-checked. So she's able to be active like she is at sixty-one.

So he thought that was funny. So he added a couple more things that happened in a lacrosse game to players. And because these things happened, they don't play anymore. But Tina Turner never got cross-checked! So it was funny to us.

Joint use

We made a treaty with England in 1701 "whereas we give to the people a parcel of land" 800 miles long, 400 miles wide, in what is now Canada.

Recently, there was a court case in Canada. And the court ruled that Native people could hunt and fish in that territory that was given to them. They didn't have to abide by the laws of Canada. They could hunt there anytime.

The last sentence in that 1701 treaty says that we, the Native people, would have the right to hunt and fish in that territory. So we didn't give them the land outright; we kept our right to that land. The treaties that we made with the state of New York also state the same thing, that we can hunt and fish in all the ceded lands. Which means we didn't give the land over totally. It was joint use so that we could then help, hopefully, protect the lands and the waters for future generations.

Bubble busters

One of the things that we have in our society is "bubble busters." Which means that anytime that you start bragging about yourself and what you're doing, we've got a pin that'll break your balloon. And so my son and I refer to it as "bubble busters." So that if someone decides it's time for him to start bragging about himself, we tell him about all those things that he did wrong and that he couldn't do. And it knocks him back down to where he's supposed to be: thankful of the gifts that he has. And you don't brag about these things.

And because of that, my sons don't talk about the awards that they have. And I talk about them all the time because I, the father, can do this. Because they're achievements of my sons. And I can say, "Well, my sons did this." And I'm proud of what they've done. And they get very uncomfortable with me. Uncomfortable that I'm out there going on about these things.

"Dad, you shouldn't be saying these things."

I say, "Well, I can do this because these are things that have happened. You've done them and I can be proud of them." But they don't like that. Because the individual who does that gets his bubble busted . . . because the rest of us start talking about all the things that he couldn't do that he tried to do, that didn't turn out.

We had this one guy. He joined our team and he had played for another team. And because he was big—well, he was an athlete—but because he was bigger than the guys he was playing with, he was kind of like a self-proclaimed star. And so he was playing with us, but he wasn't of that caliber. In fact, he was one of the lower guys.

So we're in a situation where we need a goal. "Well," he says, "what I'm going to do is I'm going to start over here; I'm going to run across." He says, "You give the ball to me and I'll score."

We all looked at each other and we kind of smirked. And so we said, "Well, we'll try it out." So he does what he said he's going to do, we give him the ball, and he doesn't score.

So after the play was over with, we tell him, "That was a good play," we say, "but next time we do this we're going to give it to someone who knows how to put the ball in the net, someone who can score!"

So we have these little things like this that. . . .

And the stories we tell are funny. There was one of our stars who was running down the sidelines. And I came up and I checked him. I knocked him down and I knocked him out of bounds. And he came up to me and he said, "Well, that was a good check."

"Well, it wouldn't have happened," I said, "if you were paying attention to what you were doing, instead of smiling at all the girls on the sidelines."

"I wasn't smiling at the girls."

I said, "If you weren't, then you wouldn't have got hit like you did."

And so we all had a laugh over that, you know, because now we were calling him "girl watcher."

Jay Leno says, "If I have to explain my joke, it's not a joke. That's bad," he says, "when you have to do that." But we can do that here. I'm not Jay Leno. And people aren't going to be able to understand some of this stuff, I think, you know. It isn't going to be funny to them. They may not catch the sarcasm that's in here, also. Because that's what I'm doing. And I can be *very* sarcastic. But I'm trying to keep it cool!

Still Indian Country

Now I'm going to talk about a treaty made between the Haudenosaunee and Great Britain in 1768. The British came into our territory about 100 years before the state of New York became the state of New York. And so we've been dealing with them for 300 years.

And they put a person in Johnstown, New York, named Sir William Johnson. He was the liaison between Great Britain and the Haudenosaunee. They built him a big mansion in Johnstown, which is still there. If you go up there you can see the mansion and see how he lived. And it's a beautiful place he had. And they have all the historical notes about what he did, meetings that he held, not only with the Mohawks, but with the other nations.

So when Great Britain wanted to make a treaty in 1768, they assigned him to be the negotiator. And we didn't hold the treaty at his place in Johnstown; we came to Fort Stanwix in what is now Rome, New York. That's where we met. And the reason for the meeting, we find out, is that Great Britain wanted to establish the western boundary of its colony called the Province of New York.

And so they set up the western boundary line of the Province of New York, the colony of Great Britain. A line was drawn from Fort Stanwix down in a southern direction and then in a southwesterly direction. And everything west of that line was "Indian Country," and not open for settlement by the people who were coming across the Atlantic Ocean to settle. So the English people were settling from the Atlantic Ocean to Fort Stanwix. That's what was open to them.

But in 1776, on July 4, these people who were moving into the territory were unsatisfied with their relationships with the King of England. And so they protested and they declared their independence. And they said, "We hold these truths to be self-evident, that all men are created equal." They are endowed with rights given to them by the Creator. And those rights are "Life, Liberty and the pursuit of Happiness."

Now these men who made this statement are the ones who wrote up the Constitution of the United States. And Article 1 of the Constitution said there would be a way of putting people into the House of Representatives by counting the people in the state. And everybody would be counted, because they were all equal, except blacks and Indians. Blacks and Indians were not equal. Therefore their statement that all men were created equal was. . . .

So anyway, this boundary line then, set up by Great Britain and the Haudenosaunee in 1768, can only be changed by those two parties. Anything after that, not authorized by Great Britain, was invalid. But starting out, this colony of Great Britain is then separated from Great Britain. And New York declared itself to be a state of the United States.

New York is recognized in the 1783 Treaty of Paris as a part of the United States, but that treaty is with the whole United States, and not just New York. Yet New York acted as if it had its own sovereignty and its own right to negotiate with those Haudenosaunee who lived west of the 1768 line. We were living as independent and separate from New York because in 1768 we made a treaty that clearly stated that New York ended at Fort Stanwix.

I know that Governor George Clinton came to the 1788 treaty with the Onondagas. And he acted as if he was representing Great Britain. And he wasn't. Because the only ones that can change that border line are Great Britain and the Haudenosaunee. And if the state of New York did not have authorization from Great Britain to negotiate a new boundary, then that treaty is illegal and invalid.

The thirteen colonies show up in 1784 at Fort Stanwix saying, "We are the United States." And they make a treaty. Now if the United States did not have authorization to act on behalf of Great Britain, specifically with regard to the terms of the 1768 treaty, they could not change that border. And the 1784 treaty does that: it changes the border lines. So if the United States didn't have the authority from Great Britain, then that 1784 treaty with the United States and the Haudenosaunee is not legal on the border lines that were changed. Which means that the state of New York remains as it was in 1768, from the Hudson River to Fort Stanwix, or Rome.

Great Britain sent over a surveyor to draw the borders of their colony. And this map remained in England for all of these years. And then it was sent from Great Britain to Canada, to one of the libraries in Canada, in the Loyalist Collection at Brock University in Ontario. And because the map is so big, they took microfilm pictures of the map in little squares.

And when the library received these microfilm documents from Great Britain, they were repairing their library. So their library wasn't open. So those papers were sitting there in the library for quite a while. And then they opened up their library. And when they did, historians were then allowed to go in and look at these papers. Two researchers who looked at these microfilm manuscripts were my friend Bob Venables, a historian who is retired from Cornell University, and his son, Brant, a graduate student in historical archaeology at Binghamton University. Now in the microfilm collection were maps. And Brant Venables found a map in the microfilm that shows the western border line of the colony of York. And it says that border is just west of Fort Stanwix. So Fort Stanwix is the last settlement in their colony. So that was the territory of the colony.

There is no doubt in our minds and in the documents kept by the British that New York and the other colonies stopped at the border drawn up at Fort Stanwix. On November 1, 1768, our speaker representing the Haudenosaunee—perhaps he was Conoghquieson; the British did not record his name—addressed Sir William Johnson. Our speaker stated that this treaty was the last cession the Haudenosaunee would make, because it was so vast. He also emphasized an important definition of the hunting rights of all Indian nations: these rights would exist as an unrestricted right on *both* sides of the boundary line, but the hunting rights of the colonists would be restricted to the colonists' side of the treaty line. This was then confirmed by a wampum belt.

Brother

Now as we have made so large a Cession to the King of such a valuable and Extensive Country, We do expect it as the Terms of our

Agreement that strict regard be paid to all our reasonable desires—We do now on this[,] on behalf and in the name of all our Warriors of every Nation, condition that all our Warriors shall have the liberty of hunting throughout the Country as they have no other means of subsistance [sic] and as your people have not the same occasions or inclinations—That the White people be restricted from hunting on our side of the Line to prevent contensions [sic] between us[, and we record this agreement in] A [wampum] Belt.

Now that colony then became, I presume, the state of New York. So the state of New York is from the Hudson River to Fort Stanwix or Rome. That's it. Anything beyond that has to be changed by Great Britain and the Haudenosaunee, in order to change that border line. And since that wasn't done, the New York State border line ends at Rome, New York.

And since the border line of New York stops at Rome, New York, that means that the treaty between the United States and the Haudenosaunee, which moved that border line to the Mississippi River—because it took in the Ohio Valley, Indiana, Illinois, Kentucky, Tennessee, and so forth—that treaty is illegal. And the Ohio Valley is not part of the United States. It still belongs to the Haudenosaunee and other Indian nations.

New York State commissioned Edward Everett to investigate the status of New York Indians. So he made out his report, called the Everett Report, in 1922. He submitted it to the New York State Assembly. The assembly looked at it and would not accept it. They would not accept it because Edwards, in his research, found out that all of that land west of Rome still belonged to the Haudenosaunee.

And once, they published the Everett Report—part of it, some of it. They did not show the information that allowed Edward Everett to draw his conclusion that the land still belonged to the Indians. So since that time we've been looking for the rest of the report. Lulu Stillman, who was the secretary to Edward Everett, wrote to us and told us the page number which had this information.

And we looked at the copy of the Everett Report that we had. And our pages didn't go that high. Which means that some of the Everett Report was not published. And so we've been looking for this information for a number of years. And when these researchers went into that library in Canada and found this map that was dated 1772, it showed Fort Stanwix is the last settlement in their colony, which means New York State ended at Rome, New York.

The map that we have shows 1772 and that border. And on the map there's a stamp by the Queen of England, indicating that this map is an authentic document showing the border line of the Colony of York. And if the people of New York, who separated from Great Britain, decided to claim their territory as the state of New York, it ends at Rome.

And these people then, in 1776, separate themselves from Great Britain. And then they show up at a meeting with the Haudenosaunee, supposedly representing Great Britain and going to change that border line. And I don't think they had the authority to do that. So none of those treaties after 1768 have the authorization from Great Britain to sit down and negotiate new borders.

So the border of the state of New York runs from the Hudson River to Rome, New York. And anything west of there is Indian Country. So anything west of Rome, New York, is not part of the United States.

Therefore the United States doesn't exist per se, because their border starts at the Mississippi River and goes west. Between Rome and the Mississippi River is land that still belongs to the Haudenosaunee and other Indian nations, as documented by Edward Everett in 1922 and as documented by the map made by England in 1772.

Of course all of this information I just gave out is *all* documented and I can produce the documents: I can produce the map; I can produce a statement that says that Governor Clinton lied to the Haudenosaunee when he said he represented a continuation of a central government that is represented by the Covenant Chain. He didn't. But I have all of these documents, so I can document everything that I said. And if you don't believe me, you can go back, you can check. Because the documents are there.

And if you want to rebut what I say, then you have to produce a letter from Great Britain that says Governor Clinton was authorized by Great Britain to negotiate a treaty with us at Fort Stanwix. And if those papers don't exist, then all of those treaties are illegal. And my statement stands, that New York State ends at Rome, and everything west of Rome to the

Mississippi, belongs to the Haudenosaunee, as verified by Edward Everett in his report to the New York State Assembly in 1922.

Also, in 1861, Franklin Hough submitted a report containing all the documents from New York's Commissioners of Indian Affairs. This report came from his committee, established by legislation, whose purpose was to extinguish Indian title to the land west of Rome. It was submitted to the courts in the Cayuga land claims in 1999. Lots of copies were made and distributed to all of the parties involved in the land case. The report tells of the meetings between the committee and members of the Haudenosaunee, but it does not claim that the committee accomplished their mission to extinguish title. Therefore, the Haudenosaunee still have title to the lands from Rome to Mississippi, as per the 1772 map. It is still Indian Country.

Living by the natural laws

Earlier, I talked about living under the natural laws. There is an unwritten law—among our people anyway, told to us by our fathers—that when you go hunting, you only go out for what is necessary. And you only take what you need. So that whatever you're hunting will then be able to continue on into the future.

Now I grew up this way; Oren grew up this way. And I used to go down to Oren's house and say, "Let's go hunting pheasants." He'd say, "All right."

So he would go get his gun that once belonged to his father. It was a twelve-gauge shotgun with no trigger. So to fire the gun, you had to pull the hammer back, and let the hammer go, in order to fire a shot. But Oren was so used to this gun that when a pheasant went up, he would pull the hammer back, take aim, let go of the hammer, and shoot the pheasant. And when he went hunting with me, he only took one shell. Because that's all he needed, was one pheasant.

And so we would go out. He would shoot a pheasant; I would shoot a pheasant. And we were all done hunting and we would come home. Or we'd shoot a rabbit, or whatever. Something for dinner.

One day we had the opportunity to go hunting with one of the people who had moved into the territory. (For clarification, we refer to these people as "white people.") So anyway, we were out hunting with this guy. And so we show up at the field. He's got a box of shells. Now a box of shells—that means he's got twenty-five shells because they come in a box of twenty-five.

So Oren had a box of shells at home, maybe. Maybe not. But out of this box he took one shell. I had one shell in my jacket, in my pocket. And I was thinking when I saw this guy with a box of shells, *What the heck is he going to do with twenty-five pheasants?* Because that's what we were hunting.

We decided that Oren would get the first shot. I would get the second. And if we saw another one, then the white guy would get the third one. So we went out.

Now this man had dogs. And Oren and I were not used to hunting with dogs. Hunting with dogs gives you an advantage, because the dog tells you there's a pheasant ahead of you. And then you say, "Flush." And the dog jumps, and the bird goes up. But you *know* the bird is going to go up.

The way Oren and I hunted, we would just walk through and we would come across a pheasant. And he would go up. And we had no idea that there was a pheasant there. So, it was a big surprise. And you had to get over your surprise, level your gun, and then shoot before the bird got out of range.

So anyway, we encountered a pheasant. The pheasant went up in the air. Oren pulled the hammer back on his twelve-gauge and fired a shot. And the bird came down. He had a string; he tied the bird to his belt. And we went on.

And another pheasant went up. And this was my turn, so I shot. And the pheasant came down. I took out a string and tied his legs up and tied it to my belt. So I had my pheasant. And as far as Oren and I were concerned, we were done hunting.

But the guy with the box hadn't fired yet. He had a pump gun and his was the next bird. So a bird flew up. This man fired *seven* shots at this bird and never hit it. So we went on further and encountered another pheasant. And he shot seven times at that one. Now he had shot *fourteen* times and still didn't have a bird. So a third one went up and he did the same thing. With this pump gun, he was able to just pump shots out, one right after another at a rapid pace.

And he put seven more shots in the air and didn't get a bird. So I said to myself, *Well, I see why he brings twenty-five shells.* He has shot twenty-one times and he doesn't have a bird yet. He's got four more shells, and if it takes seven to shoot at one bird and he's only got four left, he's going to have to change his style in order to get a pheasant.

Anyway, a bird went up and he did get it. So we were all done hunting. He said, "Are we going to hunt some more?"

I said, "No, that's all. One pheasant is all we need. Under the natural laws, that's all you hunt."

And it was a lesson. I remember that one day, and I remember it when I see movies of people who have a fight. And cops and robbers. And the cops and the robbers are shooting at each another with their pistols. They don't hit each other; they're just shooting. They shoot everything in sight, except each other. They hit trees; they hit the wall, windows. And as these movies went on, one shot was not enough. They wanted to come in and shoot as many as they could, so they got machine guns. And the machine guns were the same way. They came in with a machine gun and would shoot hundreds of shots and never hit anything. And that didn't matter: it was that they got off all of those shots. Same as this guy that we were hunting with.

And I see that the wars are the same way. They have machine guns, they have guns that fire rapidly, big guns. And they shoot. It doesn't matter whether they hit anything. It's the idea that they got a shot off. Totally different concept in fighting and usage of weapons. One shot is all you need to do what you want to do, if you're accurate. But they didn't care whether they were accurate or not. They were just happy and content to shoot fifty shots at something. Didn't matter whether they hit it or not.

And in the early 1600s when we met with the Dutch people and we told them that you live under the natural laws, these are part of the laws that we told them. In order to make sure that we go on into the future, we have to have animals, for food. So when you hunt, only shoot what you need when you need it. When you go fishing, take only what you need when you need it.

The animals do the same thing. A bear will go fishing. He'll stand in the river and when the salmon or the fish jump out of the water to clear the falls, he'll catch one. And then he'll come back and he'll eat. And then he's all done. He doesn't stand there and eat all of the fish that are coming up. He only takes what he needs.

So these are the natural laws that you're supposed to be living under. And unfortunately, that has not happened.

And so the State passed laws that limit what you can take. I was at work one day and this hunter said to me, "Boy," he said, "I wish I was an Indian."

I said, "Why?"

He said, "Well, you can hunt and fish anytime you want, right?"

I said, "Right."

"Well," he said, "if I had that right, I'd be hunting all the time."

And I said, "Well, you've been hunting this year. You've been hunting for deer. Right?"

He said, "Yes."

I said, "You have a license to shoot one deer." I said, "How many have you shot?"

He said, "Seven."

"That's why you have laws," I said. "I don't have laws. I can go out and hunt anytime I want," I said, "because when I go hunting, I'll only shoot one. And that's the law that we live by. And it's not written down; it's a spoken law. You have a written law and you get a license to shoot *one*. And with that license you've shot seven. If you were not required to have a license," I said, "your people could be out every day. And within a short time there might be no deer left. They would have killed them all, like they did with the buffalo. They almost drove them into extinction, by shooting them," I said, "and if your people had those rights that I have, there would be no rabbits; there would be no pheasants; there would be no deer, because you'd be out there every day, shooting. And then not using them."

So it's important to notice that when I speak about natural laws, these are the laws I talk about. "And," I said to him, "these are the laws that were explained to the Dutch people in the early 1600s. Coming into our territory, *you can live here as long as you live by the natural laws*. You will not pollute the water. You will make sure that the water will continue to be fresh for the next generation. There will be animals for the next genera- tion. There will be plants and medicines for the next generation, and that is the way we continue today."

I said, "If you're talking to someone like Jake Swamp, and he tells you that he's going out to get medicine, he will go out into the woods. He will find the medicine that he needs, but he won't pick it. And he won't pick it because it may be the last one. It needs to reproduce so that the medicine will continue to live. So he goes and looks for another one. And when he finds more, those are the ones he'll pick. But he won't pick the first one because, for all he knows, it might be the last one. So he will never pick the last one, because that would stop the growth of that medicine."

These are the natural laws that we talked about in the early 1600s.

The Haudenosaunee:
a union of sovereign nations

Although physically situated within the territorial limits of the United States today, Native nations like the Onondaga Nation and the other members of the Haudenosaunee retain their status as sovereign nations. Like the United States, the Haudenosaunee is a union of sovereign nations joined together for the common benefit of its citizens.

It is governed by a Grand Council of Chiefs—fifty chiefs—who deliberate and make decisions for the people concerning issues both domestic and international. The Haudenosaunee began as a group of sovereign nations aligned to deal with other Native nations surrounding their lands. Later, it was the body that negotiated with Europeans when the latter came into their territories beginning in the early 1600s.

Sovereignty has been a big issue with us for a long time, but the chiefs before us were unable to handle it, because they didn't have command of the English language. They could explain in Onondaga their feelings about this, but they could not transfer it over to English so that authorities outside of the territory would understand what they meant or how it was. Also, there were no organizations for civil liberties that could assist them in straightening out the situation or solving the problem that we were having.

Growing up as a teenager, I remember the sheriffs being here in Onondaga. And they would come in and they would arrest our people on New York State laws. And we knew when they were going to do this because our people got arrested during planting and harvest time. They would be walking down the street. The sheriffs would come down and arrest them for public intoxication. Then they would send them to Jamesville Penitentiary up on the other side of Jamesville, New York.

Jamesville Penitentiary was sort of self-sufficient in that they had a garden. They harvested and they fed themselves. They had cows, they had horses, they had pigs, chickens, and so forth. And they were healthy animals, mostly because it was our people who were taking care of them. When the penitentiary needed something to be done, they'd come down and arrest somebody. And then they would put them in the chicken coop or the pig pen or someplace, to take care of these animals. And we did their planting and their harvesting.

So we were the primary workers. It was just like when the United States brought over the slaves, who were the ones that were taking care of the land in Africa. And they were farmers and so forth, too. They were brought here to take care of the plantations. They knew how to farm; they took care of farms. And so the plantations grew and were prosperous because of the people that were being brought over from Africa as slaves. They were very proficient in farm work.

So they did the same thing here, only they put us—they put our people—in the penitentiaries. And I grew up that way, you know, watching. And if they needed someone—if they wanted to come here and arrest somebody—they didn't use the same format that they have in the city. In the city you need to have a search warrant and so forth before you walk into a house.

The sheriffs used to come to our place. They would kick in the door, bust it down, and go in and arrest the person. And they knew from previous experience what this person was like and how strong he was. So sometimes, when they would come to arrest somebody, they would bring three cars. In each car there were two sheriffs because it would take six sheriffs to arrest this man.

I remember this.

And then as I grew up and I was studying laws and treaties and so forth, I said, "Wait a minute, this is a whole, total violation of our sovereignty." Sovereignty means, you know, that you are the power within specified boundary lines.

Sovereignty is the state of existence as a self-governing entity. And it was in this capacity that the Onondagas and other members of the Haudenosaunee sat with delegates from England, France, and the Netherlands in the years prior to American independence. During the colonial era, the Haudenosaunee made at least fifty treaties with European powers, most of which were expressions of peace and friendship. Some were made to share land, but the member-states of the Haudenosaunee retained their hunting, fishing, and gathering rights within the territory that they agreed to open to settlers.

Colonists protesting Britain's colonial policies organized a Continental Congress in 1774 and again in 1775. After this second Continental Congress issued the Declaration of Independence in 1776, the thirteen colonies each became independent states and began to conduct themselves as sovereign governments. In order to cooperate, the new states set up the Articles of Confederation in 1781, but then changed that government to a more centralized one under the Constitution in 1787–1789. Both of these governments—the old Articles and the new Constitution—had similarities to the Haudenosaunee's, in fact, but there were also differences. For example, the Articles and the Constitution both intentionally omitted women from politics. The US Constitution specifically vested the president or his appointed representatives with the exclusive legal right to negotiate treaties, which are agreements between sovereign nations. And it gave the Senate the exclusive power to ratify those treaties. The Commerce Clause further granted Congress the exclusive authority to regulate commerce with Indian nations.

Early US statesmen acknowledged the international status of Indian nations and the treaties made with them. Rufus King, one of America's founding fathers and later a US Senator from New York, equated Indian treaties with all other international treaties, such as those with Britain or France. In a February 12, 1818 letter to his son describing an Indian treaty recently rejected by the Senate, King concluded with a telling postscript: "As all Treaties, including Indian Treaties, are deemed State Secrets, until ratified and published, you must so far regard this communication as such, as not to publish the same."

So Rufus King was one of those men who lived in the British colony of the province of New York, that is now the state of New York. He was part of that.

And the people who lived in New York were George Washington, Benjamin Franklin, Thomas Jefferson, and Rufus King. And in 1776 these are the people who declared independence on July the 2nd, that was proclaimed on July the 4th. And they did it not only for New York, but I guess they did it for all thirteen colonies. And because they did this, they then proclaimed themselves the United States. And the Province of New York became New York State.

And when they did this, they established laws. And when they were doing it, as I have mentioned, they wrote the Constitution. And these people, Thomas Jefferson, George Washington, Benjamin Franklin, and so forth, wrote in their declaration that it is self-evident that all men are created equal. And they are endowed by the Creator with inalienable rights, the right of life, liberty, and the pursuit of happiness.

With this mutual understanding as a backdrop, the United States government entered into three major treaties with the Haudenosaunee. Interestingly, two of these treaties have never been abrogated by either side and remain in effect to this day, while a third, the 1789 Treaty of Fort Harmar, was superseded by the Treaty of Canandaigua in 1794. Validation of this treaty lies in the fact that the Haudenosaunee still receive from the United States annuities—from the Canandaigua Treaty—in the form of bolts of muslin cloth and a $4,500 annuity allocated each year from the US Treasury.

In 1871, the United States ceased treaty-making with Native nations, but also declared that existing treaties would always be in effect. By that time, the United States had entered into nearly 400 legitimate treaties with Indian nations. Thus the Onondaga Nation maintains and has never relinquished either its national or collective sovereignty as a member of the Haudenosaunee. Such sovereignty was defined by the founding leader who we call the Peacemaker as belonging to those nations that accepted the Great Law; subscribed to its spiritual, moral, and social mandates; and placed themselves under the authority of the governing councils of chiefs. There has never been any provision for transferring that sovereignty to any other entity, nor have the traditional chiefs of the Haudenosaunee ever consented to such a transfer.

Now the same people who wrote the Declaration of Independence sat down and wrote the Constitution of the United States. But "all men are created equal" was forgotten when they wrote that. When they wrote the laws as to how the census would be taken so that there would be one representative for every 30,000 people who would sit in the House of Representatives, Indians and black slaves were not counted the same way. And that was because they figured that an African American slave was only a fraction of a person. Therefore, they weren't qualified to be counted the same way.

So much for "all men are created equal."

And we lived outside of the state of New York, in Indian Country. We owned land but we didn't pay taxes. Therefore we were also excluded from the count. And we still aren't included. In 1868 the Fourteenth Amendment amended that law, but article 1, section 2 of the US Constitution, where it says, "excluding Indians not taxed" was not changed. It still maintains, it still says: "excluding Indians not taxed."

So when the census is taken, the census-takers are not allowed in this territory of Onondaga. And they're not allowed in Oneida, or—I think—Mohawk territory. So it doesn't matter how many Haudenosaunee are in this state—we're not counted and therefore we don't put seats in the House of Representatives. That's how it was supposed to be done at the beginning.

So George Washington and those others decided that all men were not really created equal. They left out African Americans, the women, and the Indians. But over the years the women, because of their contact with the Onondaga women, have forged ahead and gone with women's civil rights. And there's a museum up in Seneca Falls that tells about their fight for equal rights and their right to vote.

So anyway, because this was happening in our territory right up until I became a leader in 1964, I said, "Well that's not right. They cannot come into our territory with this." So I invited the Department of the Interior, the Department of Justice, the Bureau of Indian Affairs (BIA), the County of Onondaga, the mayor of Syracuse, the state troopers, the sheriffs, and the police department of Syracuse. And they sat in the longhouse here at Onondaga. And I explained to them that their laws were only within their boundary lines. And when they came into the territory of the Onondaga, they were outside of their boundary lines. Therefore their laws did not apply. And so we have civil and criminal jurisdiction within our territory.

Like the individual states of the United States, each member nation of the Haudenosaunee retains the authority to govern its own internal affairs. Within the framework of the Great Law and its own specific laws, each individual nation reserves the right to adjudicate internal disputes, pass laws for the welfare of its own community, assess fees, regulate trade and commerce, control immigration and citizenship, oversee public works, approve land use, and appoint officials to act on its behalf. Every member of the Haudenosaunee has the authority to defend its citizens against internal and external dangers, and to advocate for the peaceful resolution of conflict, and the equitable distribution of collective resources.

Like the US federal government, the Haudenosaunee is itself a government based on laws and specific procedures, holding the power to resolve differences between member nations and to guarantee that its members are of one mind on matters of international treaties, territorial disputes, international trade, or any other issue that affects its long-term welfare. The chiefs of the Grand Council are designated advocates of peace and hold the future welfare of the people in their hands. They are empowered to deliberate, to consider all options, to arrive at consensus, and to enact laws that are added to the collective set of laws called the Great Law.

But the US federal government passed laws in 1948 and 1950. The federal laws are cited by the book that they're in. And USC [United States Code] title 25 is the book they're in. Title 25, section 232 gives the state of New York criminal jurisdiction. And section 233 gives them civil jurisdiction. And these laws are violations of the Constitution, because they don't have the right to pass laws going into another nation's territory. Since the United States didn't have civil and criminal jurisdiction in our territory, they couldn't give it to the state. So those laws are in violation of civil rights.

So I explained this to these people, and I said,

But you people have a lot of machines that fingerprint. You have photos and you have a whole database of criminals, and so forth. So you have really advanced your technology in catching those who violate the laws.

And we don't have this in our territory. So there are times when it will be necessary for us to ask for your assistance in some incident that has happened in our territory. And when we do this, we are only asking for your assistance on this one incident. So you can come in and help us, but it does not transfer jurisdiction. You can come in and help us, but you can't pass any laws. You can't violate our sovereignty, and you cannot arrest anybody.

So they all agreed. And it's been that way since that time. So since that happened, the state troopers don't come into our territory anymore. The sheriffs don't come into our territory. The city police don't come into our territory. And if they do, they have to ask permission. And this has been going on for years now. It's an example of laws being followed as they're set up.

And the United States, the state of New York, the County of Onondaga and the City of Syracuse have set up laws, they have set up courts and they have put boundary lines down for the courts.

But because of the 1768 treaty with the English, there is already a boundary line. And west of that boundary line is Indian Country. In the US Constitution they ruled that we're not taxed. We're not taxed because we're in Indian Country. So it's a recognition of that 1768 treaty. That treaty has never been appealed, never been changed, never been amended. Therefore that line still exists. And everything west of Rome is Indian Country.

And so the laws of the state of New York end at Rome. And anything beyond, west of that, is Indian Country and those laws do not apply. Therefore, we at Onondaga are the only government that regulates what goes on in our territory. The state and the federal government have tried to come into our territory and they've passed laws. And we have ignored them and we've told them that we won't abide by them.

When we found out they were passing those laws, we went down and we told them, "You can't do this because . . . ," and we gave our reasons why. And, for instance, when they were passing the civil jurisdiction law, we went down and said, "You cannot pass this law. Because if you give the state of New York this jurisdiction, they'll tax us."

And the federal government said to us, "This is not about taxation. This is a way to open up the courts so that if you have disputes, the courts will overview and settle them." That was in 1948.

In 1958, Edward Best, attorney general for the state of New York, said, "It is my opinion that we have the right to tax Indians." And so 1958 started the fight against the state of New York over taxation laws. And we've been fighting since 1958 because of that 1948 civil jurisdiction law that was passed. And we have court decisions that I have mentioned in previous presentations. One of the decisions, for instance, was with Judge Gorman when he ruled that New York State tax laws 28 and 29 are invalid, illegal, and unconstitutional in the territory of the Onondagas.

And another decision was in 1971, when a Utica judge, James Gordon, ruled that the state Department of Transportation did not have the power of eminent domain. They had to stop work and remove themselves from Onondaga territory, from constructing a third lane in our territory on Route 81.

So we have maintained this position that we are a sovereign nation within the boundary lines of the United States and the state of New York. The borderlines of our territory stop New York State and federal laws from coming into our territory. Therefore we're a sovereign nation.

In the past, the chiefs, headmen, and delegates of each nation were involved in the negotiation and acceptance of the terms of treaties with European governments, and later with the United States government. These treaties were then presented to the Grand Council for approval. If accepted, a treaty came to represent the legal relationship between the United States and the traditional nations.

Haudenosaunee sovereignty was not granted by the United States any more than US sovereignty was granted by the English Crown in the eighteenth century. The United States declared its independence as a natural right, given to people by the Creator. Sovereignty is an inherent right that, in the case of the Onondaga Nation, was established with the formation of the Haudenosaunee and adoption of the Great Law of Peace.

And we've been that way since the United States started dealing with us and the State of New York started dealing with us 300 years ago. We are recognized as a government with laws, civil and criminal, and a system where we can take care of our own disputes. Therefore we are a nation. And because we are recognized by state and federal governments as a nation, their laws do not apply in our territory.

It is very important for the people who are coming into leadership in Onondaga to understand this, so that when the state or the county or the federal government tries to come into our territory and starts passing laws that come into our territory, you have the authority and the responsibility to stop them at the border line and explain to them why they can't come into the territory. And these laws are in place and have been there for the last three or four hundred years.

The Onondaga Nation has had and continues to possess sovereign authority, both as a nation and as part of the Haudenosaunee. With such sovereignty comes the power to pass laws, make treaties, and act on behalf of the Onondaga people in relations with other sovereign nations. It is an authority that the nation and its designated representatives take very seriously.

Getting enough air

Here's something that the medical people know. And it's a good thing they do. If the people gather in a circle, a closed circle, they have the capability of sucking up all the air so there's no air in that circle. So a person falls down or faints or something and is lying on the ground. And people come to see how that person is. They form a circle around the person. And if they stand there long enough, that person is going to run out of air because they have the capability of sucking up all the air within that circle.

But when the emergency vehicle arrives, the ambulance, or the car with the medics in there—they *know* this. So the first thing that they say when they get there is, "Stand back and give them air." Meaning that they know that this person who's in the circle, lying on the ground, may suffer from lack of oxygen, because the people in the circle around him have the capability of sucking up all the air within that circle. Which brings the question, "Who are these people, anyway, that can do this?"

The Revolutionary War

Before we get into the Revolutionary War, maybe we should explain first why the Revolutionary War came about. And this came about because long before the Revolution, Benjamin Franklin, Thomas Jefferson, and the other men who would become known as the Founding Fathers of the Constitution of the United States were looking for a way in which they could govern themselves. And they said, "There's a group of people out there that have a government. We should learn about it."

And so they sent delegates out to see us. And they asked if we would come to them and explain our government and how it operated here. And we said we could do that. We said, "We'll come to you and we'll explain our government and how we operate." So in 1744 we went to Lancaster, Pennsylvania. And there, an Onondaga chief named Canassatego explained to these people the government of the Haudenosaunee.

Benjamin Franklin then printed out in his press, the Lancaster Treaty of 1744, *in* 1744. And he explained what was told to them. And we explained to them, you know, that we joined five nations together for strength. They had thirteen colonies strung out along the eastern coast. And it would be to their benefit to join the thirteen colonies together as one.

And so they listened to us. There was Thomas Jefferson, James Madison. . . . And it took them a while—like thirty-two years. And they finally decided that they would not be under England anymore. They declared themselves independent. "The Declaration of Independence" they called it in 1776, thirty-two years after we explained to them why it's better to have a government that unites all of the thirteen colonies.

And in 1775, the Revolutionary War then started between the Thirteen Colonies, here in what is now the United States, and England. But before the war started, the Thirteen Colonies got together and said that the Haudenosaunee are very powerful. They have the power to determine who will win the war between the colonists and England. And some of them are friends with England and some are our friends. But we would rather that they not be in the war itself.

And so George Morgan was commissioned by the Thirteen Colonies to go to Haudenosaunee territory and talk to them about being neutral. Now they had been with us in various stages of politics and they realized that the only way that they could talk with us was to send wampum strings—invitation wampum—and tell us what they wanted to say, at a certain place, at a certain time. So this was done.

And to show that the words that they were putting out were true, they commissioned someone to make a wampum belt. The wampum belt was 2,500 beads. It's a white belt with thirteen diamonds down the center of it in a row going across, horizontally. The thirteen diamonds represent the Thirteen Colonies. So they decided that we should meet at Fort Pitt, which is now Pittsburgh, Pennsylvania. So the Haudenosaunee went down there. There were 1,500 of us that went down there to Fort Pitt and listened to George Morgan as he presented the upcoming Revolutionary War between the thirteen colonies and Great Britain.

And they wanted us to be either fighting for them or out of the war completely. So we agreed that we would be neutral. So when the Revolutionary War started, the Haudenosaunee, politically, were neutral.

But what happened is that we had made friends on both sides. With the British—the Mohawk Joseph Brant and other Haudenosaunee, including Onondagas, were friends with the British Indian Superintendent Sir William Johnson and his family. And then we had people who were friends with colonists such as George Washington because some of our people had scouted for him during the war they call the French and Indian War [1754–63].

And so when the war broke out, those people went to help their friends. Now, the Oneidas were with the colonists and Joseph Brant was with the British. And the war went on. The War of 1812 was the last effort by England to take over the colonies. But they failed. So the colonies then became united together into what is now the United States.

After the Revolutionary War, those people who fought on the side of England had been promised that they would be taken care of. There was a treaty between England and the Thirteen Colonies. The British and the United States also sat down in 1794 and signed the Jay Treaty. And the Jay Treaty, article 3, is the only part that talks about the Native people. And it said that Native people, including the Haudenosaunee, would have free access over the borders, would not have to pay import-export taxes as they crossed and re-crossed the borders with their own personal stuff. The Natives would be able to cross the Canadian and the US border freely, without paying taxes on goods that they carried back and forth.

So at that time we had no problem entering and leaving the United States or Canada under article 3 of the Jay Treaty.

But, there's a problem out there today because of that. . . . Indians crossing that line and the new policy that's being set up on the borders, new passports, new regulations, and so forth. Canada is giving the Native people a rough time about crossing that Canadian border. They don't recognize the Jay Treaty as being their obligation because that treaty was between the United States and Great Britain, not between the United States and Canada. Therefore they don't recognize it. Anyway, that's another subject.

Anyway, after the Revolution, England said, "Well, we'll take care of you. Come up into Canada." And so a group followed Joseph Brant. They went up to what is now Ohsweken along the Grand River. And there they set up, under the Haldimand Treaty, a tract of land, starting at Lake Erie, six miles on either side of the river, all the way up to where they are. And that's a lot of territory that they had. Right now they're left with the twelve mile square, an area twelve by twelve, the rest having been lost through treaties and so forth.

But a split came, because people from all of the nations followed Joseph Brant. And when they got up to Canada, they were without the Longhouse, so to speak, you know. Because the Haudenosaunee was formed here at Onondaga. Councils were held here. The gathering of the nations was always here at Onondaga. And so when these people moved out, when they moved up into Canada, they didn't have a government like they were used to.

And so this split came. And the wampum belts were split up. And they went up there with the various languages, and they still have, to this day, kept their languages. They've got Onondaga, Cayuga, and the Mohawk language up there in this small area.

And those that remained here in the United States also were then subjected to a lot of stress. But probably the biggest stress that they were subjected to had already occurred during the Revolution, and this stress lasted long after the war. This stress was caused by the raids by John Sullivan, who was asked by General George Washington to exterminate the Haudenosaunee.

This occurred because, during the American Revolution, many Haudenosaunee allied with the British. These warriors' military successes of 1778 disturbed George Washington, who lamented the collapsing morale on the frontier and the destruction of the crops needed to feed his soldiers. In 1779 he ordered an expedition under the overall command of General John Sullivan to march into the Haudenosaunee country of what is now western New York, to knock the Haudenosaunee out of the war, and to capture Fort Niagara.

One of the things that we find out, as we read history, is this: in April 1779, the first assault of this campaign began, when 558 patriot soldiers under Colonel Goose van Schaick marched westward from Fort Stanwix, at the western end of the Mohawk River, and destroyed most of the Onondaga homes and communities, including those that were neutral or pro-patriot. It is important to note that there had been no rapes of white women at Cherry Valley or at any other frontier settlement, for, as General James Clinton noted, "bad as the Savages are,'" they never violate the chastity of any women who are their prisoners. Not so for the patriots. The patriots raped and then butchered some of our Onondaga women. This burned deep into our hearts. During a council in Niagara on December 11, 1782, Tioguanda, an Onondaga chief, recalled:

* William L. Stone, *Life of Joseph Brant—Thayendanegea, Including the Indian Wars of the American Revolution* (New York: George Dearborn, 1838), 2:404.

When They came to the Onondaga Town (of which I was one of the principal Chiefs)[,] They put to death all the Women and Children, excepting
some of the young Women that they carried away for the use of their Soldiers, and were put to death in a more shameful and Scandalous manner; Yet these Rebels calls themselves Christians.*

There was also a raid launched northward from Fort Pitt [Pittsburgh]
against some of the Senecas under General Brodhead. So there are plaques
around the state of New York that show the places where Van Schaick, Sullivan, and Brodhead went on raids and destroyed Haudenosaunee towns,
villages, and orchards in April and September 1779. So these are very
trying times for the Haudenosaunee because now they're being chased
around by the colonists.

But coming along besides this we had the introduction of the churches;
we had the introduction of rum, alcoholic beverages; we had the introduction of machinery, steel, guns. And all of these things had an effect on
what our life *used* to be. And we adapted into a different life.

We were hunters and there was a big fur trade that was available to
us. And so we were out shooting deer, bear, beaver, in order to sell our
pelts. So the introduction of these things into our territory, starting in the
1600s, was another event that changed our lives. And we have, over these
400 years, adapted to these various changes that have come to us. And
some of them, such as the boarding schools, are very traumatic.

And my dad was telling me about what the treaties were, what was
supposed to have happened: "These are the things that happened at Fort
Stanwix, Fort Harmon and Canandaigua." And he didn't have dates. He
didn't know what date that happened. He just knew there was a meeting.
And this is what happened.

Now, when you *read* about these things—and this is so interesting—
when you read what was written about our people by the historians in the

---

* Tioguanda [Tiahogwando] (Onondaga leader), speech to Allan Maclean, December
11, 1782, *The Haldimand Papers* (232 vols., hand copied from originals in the British Museum),
102:250, Public Archives of Canada, Ottawa.

1700s, those words of my dad come back. And I say, "This is what he was talking about. This is what he was telling me."

And now it's documented. Like for instance, one of the historians in the past wrote that when the Native people traveled through, you didn't know where they'd been, and you didn't know that they'd been there.

Our villages would be in a spot. We would be there for a number of years and then we would move to another spot. We set up another village, and then we would live there for a while and we'd move again. But every time we moved, you wouldn't know that we'd been there. And I was out with my dad, and I would follow behind him and you couldn't tell where he'd been. I learned to walk through the woods the same way. You couldn't tell where I'd been.

But what's here today is different. Because the homes are different. If we look back, even in the 1800s and 1900s, there were very few people. We only had 240 people. Those are all the Onondagas that we had right after the Revolutionary War because of smallpox, because of the wars, because of the people that we lost, and then the raids afterwards with Sullivan and Van Schaick. There were only 240 Onondagas—very few of us left—and from that we've grown.

And if this smallpox hadn't come in and there wasn't a Revolutionary War, we'd probably have millions of Haudenosaunee around.

All of the treaties are still in effect— they're international treaties

But then the wars continued. We had the War of 1812. And the United States and Great Britain met again in Belgium, in a village called Ghent— Ghent, Belgium—in 1815. And because of the skirmishes between the two peoples, it's understood by the people that once that happens, treaties and agreements are nullified or changed and maybe not recognized anymore.

Well, at Ghent, the United States and Great Britain restored all of the principles and the status of the Indians from whenever right up until 1811. Article 7 of this treaty says that all of our statuses are restored. Which meant that all of the treaties were still in effect and that we, because of our status, were sovereign nations. So that's an important treaty to know about. And a lot of the people—the US citizens—don't know about these treaties. They don't know about the obligations. But that's an important one because what it does is it makes all of the treaties that we've made with the United States, Great Britain, France—and earlier with the Dutch—*international treaties* since they're made between sovereign nations. The Haudenosaunee were sovereign and are *still* sovereign. As such, those treaties can be looked at by the United Nations.

I have to go talk to the animals

When I was trying to decide what should go in this book, I said to myself, *Well, I want to talk about international treaties.* Because international treaties are so important, not only for today and how we exist, but for the future. And if we don't take care of Mother Earth and the things that are here, we are not going to survive. We need fresh water, clean water; we need clean air; we need animals; we need to take care of these things. There's total disregard for this in the effort to do various things. Like there is a group of people from the DEC [the New York State Department of Environmental Conservation] who are trying to eliminate the birds that eat the fish up at Oneida Lake, those cormorants. They've been out there; they've been shooting them; they've been scaring them away—they've been trying to eliminate them.

What they did not do before they did this was to find out the purpose of these birds.

When the Creator made Mother Earth, he put down things that we would enjoy and that would help us sustain life. And everything has a purpose, no matter what it is—mostly to be part of a food chain. The people from the DEC are trying to remove these birds. And I don't think they've really done their research as to what would happen if these birds no longer existed. They could remove the birds and they might then lose the fish that they're trying to protect. Because the birds have something to do with the fish. So you have to look at all of these things.

Now, I'll give you an example of this. A man knocked on my door. And he said, "I'm from the Boy Scouts. I was looking at your hillside. It's a beautiful place." He said, "Every year we have an annual Boy Scout camping trip." He said, "I've got about 300 boy scouts I'd like to bring in and put them up on your hillside there. We'd be there for a couple of weeks," he said, "and we'll clean it up afterwards. We'll make sure everything is all nice when we get through."

And I said, "Well, before I say yes to that, I have to go talk to the animals."

He said, "What do you mean?"

I said, "Well, you're going to put 300 ten-year-old boy scouts up there. They're going to be in their house. And before I do that, I've got to talk to them, make sure it's okay. Because 300 kids running around in their house is going to disrupt their life. And I'm not sure whether they're going to agree to that."

He said, "You're going to do what?"

I said, "I'm going up to talk to the animals and see whether it's okay for you to bring 300 boys up into their house."

So he thought about it a while. He said, "I changed my mind. I withdraw my request," he said, "I see what you're talking about now."

I said, "Well, very good."

So he left without an answer. But I said, "Well, if we're going to do things that are going to disrupt the natural world, then we should be talking to the natural world." Now we used to be able to do that a long time ago. *We* did, anyway. We could talk with the animals.

A long time ago we used to be able to talk with the animals

I talked to one of the elders one day and I said, "Where do we get the songs from anyway?"

He said, "The animals gave them to us. A long time ago we used to be able to talk with the animals."

And I said, "Wow."

And one day in the longhouse we were talking about our ability to talk with the animals. And he said, "We can't do that anymore."

And I said, "Well, *we* can't." But one day my dad called me up and he said, "Come on over to the house and bring your camera."

So I said, "All right." So I went in the backyard and he was standing there by the tree.

I said, "What's up?"

He said, "Look up in the tree." There was a raccoon up there. And my dad started talking Onondaga to this raccoon. The raccoon came down the tree. And my dad was telling him, you know, that they were friends. And he had food for him.

And so the raccoon came down—and I've got pictures of this in my house. And there was a big branch that went out of the tree. The raccoon came down and sat on that branch. And my dad talked to him. And then the raccoon stood up on his hind legs and he high-fived my dad. I have a picture of the raccoon and my dad touching hands. Then the raccoon ate the food my dad had put there. And then it left.

And that's how it used to be, but my dad was able to do that. And too bad we've lost that.

"Listening" to events

A lot of the people who go to the World Series or to concerts, football games, and so forth, all they do is scream and holler from the time they get there until the time they leave. They go to a concert—say Rod Stewart is there—the announcer comes out and makes the announcement that Rod Stewart is going to be there today. And the people start screaming and hollering. And Rod Stewart comes out to say hello, and nobody can hear what he's saying. Because he gets drowned out by the people who are attending the concert, with their hollering and screaming.

And then he says he's going to sing a song. And he gives the name of the song, but you don't hear what song he's going to sing. And then he starts to sing. And when he starts to sing, the volume of noise goes up and you cannot hear his song. You cannot hear him sing. And when he finishes, they applaud and clap and holler some more. And then they applaud when he leaves the stage. But all they do is scream and holler.

And you go to a football game and the roar is so loud at this game that the coaches cannot hear themselves communicate on their phones that they need to talk about what kind of plays they want to do or how they want to act defensively. Because so many people go to concerts, football games, or events and all they do is scream and holler. Who are these people, anyway, that don't even listen to what's going on at the event?

Reluctant chiefs

Even though we spent a lot of time explaining our government to those who wrote the American Constitution, there are *vast* differences between our politics and theirs. And I don't know what happened in the translation, but our leaders are not elected. And we don't campaign to become a chief. In fact most of us don't want to be a chief.

Our process is that a clan mother will pick a person to be a leader. And they go through a process of acceptance. And then they go through a day-long ceremony called a Condolence Ceremony where that person is then installed as a chief. (I use the word "chief" because that's the accepted word for the translation of the word that we use, which is *hoya·neh*. And hoya·neh means "a man of good mind." It doesn't mean "chief.") But that's how we do that.

So when I was asked to be one of the leaders by the clan mother, I said to the clan mother, "No, I can't do that." I said, "I'm not qualified. There are certain things that I can't do that I should be able to do as a leader."

She said, "Don't worry about that. When you get in there, they'll teach you. And you'll learn."

So I refused three times before I was finally put in and I went through the ceremony that made me one of the leaders of the Haudenosaunee. And it's not a position I . . . and I had never even thought about being one of the leaders.

Whereas in your society, some of your people are born and they say, "Well, I'm going to be a senator." "I'm going to be a congressman." "I'm going to be an assemblyman," or "I'm going to be president." You know, they have visions of being in the political world. And in our community, that's not something that we think about.

My cousin Oren and I were put in, installed, in the same ceremony. And he got put in the same way that I did, you know. They asked him and he said no, as well. They finally convinced him to become one of the leaders. They kind of convinced me to be one of the leaders. And so we've been sitting there since 1964.

And a clan mother can remove me, if I do certain things. In your society you have your impeachment process. And I'm not sure how that works, but that's the process you have. In our society, a political leader can be removed by a woman. The clan mother can come up and say to the leader, "You are not conducting yourself in the manner in which you were put in there to do. And because of this I'm removing you from your position." And through this process they get removed.

Sales tax laws are illegal, invalid, and unconstitutional

Oneida Nation is having trouble with the state of New York over their territories and so forth. They've got land claims in. And the state is trying to enforce, in the territories of our people, their sales tax laws.

And in 1966, I argued with the state about these sales tax laws. And I had our lawyer contact the attorney general of the state, Louis Lefkowitz, and ask him if he would entertain the issue of this sales tax in the courts.

And Louis said, "Yes."

So we went into court in Syracuse. And much to the surprise of Louis Lefkowitz, he lost. Because we went in there on treaties, international laws, and so forth. And we said that we have territories; we have boundaries recognized by the United States, and recognized by the treaties. And the state of New York cannot come into our territory with their laws.

Now the judge, Judge Gorman, agreed with us. And he ruled that New York State sales tax laws were illegal, invalid, and unconstitutional.

And so Louis said, "Well, I can't have that. I'll appeal it."

So he appealed it and we went to Rochester to the Appellate Division. And Judge Henry ruled that Judge Gorman was correct, but that he left out some stuff. So Judge Henry made it stronger. Louis then was horrified, you know, that he had lost in both courts. And so he said he was going to appeal *that* court decision.

But he never did. And there are rules and regulations as to how you do this. And he failed to do it. So eight years later, we got a letter from Louis that said he was not going to appeal those cases. So those two court cases still stand. And those sales tax laws in the Territory of Onondaga are illegal, invalid, and unconstitutional.

When the City of Sherrill decided that they wanted to tax the Oneidas, they ended up in court. And it went through the various lower courts, but it ended up in the Supreme Court. And the Supreme Court is established by article 3 of the Constitution of the United States. And article 3 also establishes its boundaries and its jurisdiction. The Supreme Court can rule on treaties only on one issue: whether or not that treaty violates the Constitution of the United States. If it doesn't, the treaty is an okay treaty. But that's the only issue that they can rule on.

So anyway, the Supreme Court was looking at this tax issue between Sherrill and the Oneidas. And in 2005 they ruled that Sherrill could tax the Oneidas.

And I said, "Wait a minute. That's a violation of a treaty and it's a violation of the Constitution of the United States."

That's why it's important for people—our people and the citizens of the United States—to understand that there are treaties and there are treaty obligations. And maybe if they knew that, the Supreme Court would not have ruled like they did. Because of what they ruled, they violated article 2 and article 3 and article 6 of the Constitution of the United States. Plus, they violated an international treaty between the Haudenosaunee and Great Britain made in 1768.

Everything west of that line was Indian Country

Here at Onondaga and among the other Haudenosaunee, we repeat things so people don't forget. So I'm doing that now. To explain how the Supreme Court violated these things: in 1768 the United States and Great Britain sat down. And because the people who were coming across the water and settling in our territory were running out of land, they were moving across the country. We said, "You can't be doing that, because this is our territory."

And Great Britain agreed with us. In 1768, Sir William Johnson, ambassador for England, lived up in Johnstown, New York. There's a museum up there. You can go up there and see his place, see where he lived. He sat down with the Haudenosaunee and drew a line from Rome, New York, down to the Ohio and then almost to the Mississippi. Other treaties were made in the South with the Creeks and Cherokees by another ambassador, John Stuart, and these treaties set lines too. And the treaty established that everything east of Rome was open for settlement by those people that were coming across the waters. Everything west of that line was Indian Country.

Now in 1787 when the Constitution of the United States was written, the people who were sitting down to write it understood that those treaties had taken place. They understood there was a place called "Indian Country." And it wasn't open for settlement. So as they wrote how their government was going to work, they had decided that there would be two legislative bodies: the Senate and the House of Representatives.

Excluding Indians non-taxed

The Senate would have two representatives from each state. The House of Representatives would be determined by the amount of people in the state. Now in the case of New York, because of that property line, there was a difference. Not everybody was counted. And article 2 of the Constitution says, periodically—that was every ten years—a census is taken. And they will count the people, to determine how many people will sit in the House of Representatives, *excluding Indians non-taxed*, blacks, and women.

Now, in our view, we have a responsibility to the land, and we share it with the other beings placed here by the Creator. But our white brothers define this as "property" that is "owned," so we use "owned" in English even though it isn't what we would mean in our own way. And the people who were in between the ocean and that line that we drew in 1768 were property "owners." And they *do* pay tax to the state, property tax.

On the other side of that line were Indians who owned land, but didn't pay tax. So we were "Indians non-taxed." We "owned" land, but we didn't pay taxes. And because we didn't pay tax, and we were not citizens, we weren't counted. So the federal government, when they wrote the Constitution, recognized that 1768 treaty, and that line. And everything west of that was Indian Country.

The Supreme Court cannot change a treaty

But the Supreme Court justices didn't understand or don't know about or ignored that 1768 treaty between the Haudenosaunee and England. And they ignored that article 2 of the Constitution. They ruled that Sherrill could collect taxes. Now they're collecting taxes in Indian Country, which is outside of their boundary lines. Their jurisdiction has determined that they can rule in the United States. The United States does not extend into Indian Territory. So when they ruled, they went outside of their jurisdiction. Their decision is void.

It is void because it violates article 2 which determines who is counted, article 2 which recognizes the treaty and "Indians not taxed." Also it violates article 3 which formed the Supreme Court and its jurisdiction in the United States. And since they went outside the United States, it's void, because they're outside their jurisdiction.

They're violating articles 2, 3, and also article 6.

Article 6 says that any treaty that the United States has made, or will make in the future, will be supreme law of the land. Which means that the court system is underneath the treaties. And the courts cannot change a treaty. So when the Sherrill decision was decided, they changed, or they *attempted* to change the status of the Oneidas, which is a violation of the Constitution and the treaties. Therefore, null and void.

The trees know who I am

Now let's take a break from our treaty discussion for a while and talk about spiritual matters.

My world is not like your world, in that when I'm given a name, there's a ceremony. The ceremony is held at a specific time, according to the moon. And during the larger ceremony it is part of, there is a day specified for giving names. And I don't know exactly how old I was, but I was a young child. I might've been only a couple of months old, because I was born in September and the ceremony usually comes up in January. So I might have been only a few months old or it might've been two years later. I don't know. I just know that I did have a ceremony.

At that time, I was given the name of Tsa'degaihwade' of the Wolf Clan. After they gave me the name, I was held up in the longhouse and it was announced to the world that from this day forward, the world would know who I am as Tsa'degaihwade' of the Onoñda'gegá' Wolf Clan. And so whenever I go into the woods, all the trees know who I am, all the plants know who I am, and all the animals know who I am, because I was introduced at this ceremony to the world. And "to the world" means to the animals, the trees, the plants, the medicines. . . . So if I get sick and I need a medicine, they go to the medicine. And they say to the medicine, "You are now going to fulfill your duties as a medicine and you're going to Tsa'degaihwade', to help him to get better."

The plant knows exactly where it's going and to whom because of the ceremony I had when I was given my name. And because of this, I have noticed that when I leave to go somewhere—I leave the house and go out—the crows tell everybody that I am outside of the house and I am going somewhere. So I leave, and as I'm traveling to where I'm going, hawks will come down and encircle my car. And as I pass from Onondaga into Cayuga territory, there will be a hawk sitting at that border, watching me as I go by. And as I pass from Cayuga into Seneca territory, there will be a hawk sitting at *that* border, watching me as I go by. And I will also see deer as I travel along. So when I see the hawk and the deer, I know that the animals know that I am out.

Now, to take this even further, Oren Lyons and I had to go to Seattle, Washington to speak on behalf of a Lakota who was being tried on charges that they alleged to have occurred at Wounded Knee. So when I left the house—when I came out of my house to travel—the crows told everybody that I was leaving. And, as I was traveling to the airport, the hawks came and flew over my car as I traveled, to make sure I was alright. So we got on a plane and we flew to Seattle, Washington. We landed at the airport. We got in a taxicab and we went to the federal building in Seattle. And when we got out of the taxicab there in Seattle, the crows announced my safe arrival. And I could hear them: I could hear the crows telling everybody that I had arrived.

This, I know, does not usually happen in your life, but it happens in mine.

So, if you go back and review Leon Shenandoah's book, *To Become a Human Being,** you'll understand what I'm talking about. Because he says that a human being is a spiritual person, and that to be a human being, you have to be spiritual.

I'm only telling you this because it shows my connection to the world: I'm connected to the trees, to the plants, to the medicines, to the animals, to the birds, and the fish in the waters. So wherever I go, I know I am with relatives. And so it's impossible for me to walk alone in the forest.

When the people in the outside world are clearing a parcel of land for development—a business, a house, a mall, or whatever—they don't have a ceremony for all of the lives that they are taking. However, as I have already mentioned, when we take the life of a medicine, we tell the plant where it is going to go and who it is going to heal. And later I will tell you

---

* Steve Wall, *To Become a Human Being: The Message of Tadodaho Chief Leon Shenandoah* (Charlottesville, VA: Hampton Roads, 2001).

about the ceremony we had for a tree whose life we were taking, in order to make drums.

These are examples of how everything in our life is connected. The stories that I tell are all connected to each other. So if we put all the stories together, they become not individual stories, but one whole story. And that story tells me who I am. And later I'll tell you about my father and Oren Lyons at Otisco Lake. That is what my father was telling Oren, too. So when you look at that story, you understand that there are many things that we are, other than the names that we have.

These stories show, you know, that what we do is being witnessed by the spiritual world. People need to recognize that our connection to the spiritual world and the environment is important. All of the gifts that the Creator has given us are important.

I have the name Tsaʔdegaihwadeʔ that was given to me when I was, let's say, two years old. Then in 1964 when they set me up as a leader, they had a ceremony that officially put me in that position. And when I was given the title for that position, I became leader of the Beaver Clan. And the leader's name is Dehatgahdoñs, which means "man looking." It means I'm watching everything; I'm looking at both sides.

On the Condolence Cane on the Onondagas' section, which starts with the nineteenth leader of the Haudenosaunee, you've got the Thadodahoʔ, someone else, and Dehatgahdoñs. I am the twenty-first symbol on the Condolence Cane. The symbol shows two faces: one facing one way, and the other one facing the other way. So that's what my name means.

But anyway, I have two names, one that was given to me and one as a title. And because I've been given these names, the world—meaning the trees, the plants, the animals, and so forth—know me as such. So I am known to the world—not *your* world, *my* world. The trees know who I am. The plants know who I am. The animals know who I am. And the crow always announces to everybody when I leave my house. I walk out and I can hear the crows.

But I was really surprised when I got out of the taxi at Seattle, Washington, and the crows were there telling everybody that I had arrived safely. And this is part of the spiritual world that the Onondagas and the Haudenosaunee live in.

The only ones who can change a treaty are those who made it

When they wrote up the Constitution, they knew that in the future there were going to be treaties. There were going to be negotiations with foreign nations. And so article 6 of the Constitution says that all treaties made or to be made will be supreme law of the land. This means that the judicial system cannot change a treaty. And so they also set up a judicial system. So if you look at the Constitution of the United States, article 3, section 1 sets up the Supreme Court system and the judicial system that you have for your city court, county court, state courts, and so forth. And they're limited in their jurisdiction. It defines what these courts can do.

And the Supreme Court could listen to cases about treaties, but only to see whether the treaty violated the Constitution of the United States. It did not give them authority to change the provisions of the treaty.

But in 2005, the Supreme Court ruled that the town of Sherrill could go into Ray Halbritter's territory of the Oneidas and tax their territory. And I said, "Wait a minute, that's a violation of the 1768 treaty. The Supreme Court did not have that authority."

And if you look at the Constitution, how it's written, you'll also find that you come to the same conclusion, that the Supreme Court does not have the right or the authority to change a provision of a treaty, an international treaty. The only ones who can change a treaty are those that made it. The only ones who can change that treaty are the ones who went down to Fort Stanwix. So if we're going to change the status of [the land] west of that line that was drawn in 1768, England and the Haudenosaunee would have to sit down and redefine those treaties. The Supreme Court cannot do that.

But they did, in 2005, when they ruled against the Oneidas. That decision is invalid, illegal, and unconstitutional.

So it's important for us as Native people to understand the treaties and the *intent* of the treaties. And to teach the US citizens about these treaties, so that they understand that they have obligations to their treaties that are still in effect.

One mind

When we sit in council, we have an expression among our people that you can read about. There's a book out called *Words That Come before All Else.*[*] This is our Thanksgiving Address that we state *every* time we meet. Every time we have a meeting we go through a Thanksgiving Address.

And in the process of giving thanks, we mention something like the strawberries. And the strawberries were given to us by the Creator for us to eat, to give nourishment to our body. But also to make a drink out of them. So we have a strawberry drink that we use at ceremonies. And because of these ceremonies and things that we have in place, we continue to function in a manner that's over 2,000 years old.

These were put down to us and it was said that this is the way you will conduct yourself. This is the way you will be. This is how you will act, react, and so forth. And in these words that come before all others, when we're talking about the strawberries and we are giving thanks to the strawberries for still being here and providing us with food and a drink, we say, "Let us put our minds together as one and give thanks."

That means we're all thinking the same thoughts that this is what we will do. And so when we sit in council, we have that same kind of thinking. For the benefit of our people, "Let us put our minds together as one."

Now in council we have three groups: we have the Well, the Opposite Side, and the Firekeepers. And as we pass the topic around among the

* Haudenosaunee Environmental Task Force, *Words That Come before All Else: Environmental Philosophies of the Haudenosaunee* (Akwesasne Mohawk Territory: Native North American Travelling College, 1999).

three of them, the Well will say, "We have agreed upon the issue and this is what we have decided. And we send this over to you, the Opposite Side, to see whether you agree with us."

The Opposite Side will then deliberate what was passed over. And then they will say, "We have become of one mind. And we send back to you what you sent to us. And we agree with you."

The Well, then, will send it to the Firekeepers through that same process. And when we get through all three groups, we are of the same mind and we all agree on this issue. This is what we presented in 1744.

But the United States did not agree with that process. They said they would go by a vote. They said that 51 percent "yes" will defeat 49 percent "no." But this promotes a *division* between the people. Because now you've got 49 percent of the people who are not happy with the situation.

I'll give you an example. We're going to paint the wall. "Well, let's paint it black."

"No, let's paint it white."

No, we can't agree on black or white. So we mix the two together, black and white, and we get gray. We paint the wall gray. We've satisfied the black and we've satisfied the white because the wall is black *and* white, but it's gray. And we collectively agree that we will mix the black and white together to form a paint that the wall will be painted. Now we have 100 percent all agreed that this is what we will do.

You say that you're going to do something and you vote on it. And 51 percent say, "We'll do it this way." And then that's the way it gets done. Which means you've got 49 percent of the group disagreeing with what's being done. And they're not satisfied. They're not happy.

Whereas we came together as one and we're all satisfied. We're all in agreement, "This is what we will do." So there's no disagreement between us.

Your society has not done that. And still today they argue over these issues, as to who's going to do what, and how they're going to do it. So the Democrats do it and the Republicans are mad. Or the Republicans do it and the Democrats are mad. They're not working together as one.

And that's what they're supposed to be doing as leaders of their country. They're supposed to be working together *as one* for the welfare of the people. And they fail to do that. They want to be the one that waves the flag and says, "I did this," or, "We did this. The Republican Party did this and the Democrats had nothing to do with it. This is our project; this is *our* thing, so we want the people to congratulate *us* on a job well done. And the Democrats have got nothing to do with it."

We don't have that in our politics.

The Three Sisters and the food that grows out in the woods

Long ago, Onondagas developed their own food system to survive. The Haudenosaunee were hunters as well as gatherers. The crops that were the basis for our diet were corn, beans, and squash. Corn, beans, and squash are commonly referred to by the Onondaga, as well as all of the Haudenosaunee, as the "Three Sisters." These were the three foods first given to us from our Mother Earth. The corn can be dried to then be made into soup. It is also ground into flour to make a "mush" or boiled to make a bread. The corn, beans, and squash are so special to the community that they were given songs. These songs are sung to give thanks that the Three Sisters are still doing their duty and providing for us.

As I mentioned a while back, there's a book out called the *Words That Come Before All Else.* And it's an English version of our Thanksgiving Address that we use. Every time we have a meeting we give thanks to everything that the Creator has given to us. We start by acknowledging the people, their health; and then Mother Earth; and then the trees, the plants, the bushes; and then we go into the foods. And the foods that he has given to us, that are spoken of in that book, are the Three Sisters—the corn, beans, and squash. What is not mentioned is the stuff that grows that's not domesticated, that doesn't grow in the garden. It grows out in the woods.

The springtime brings these other life-sustaining foods to the Onondagas. The earliest of these are the wild onions, the dandelions, the leek, and the milkweed. These foods are sought after in the fields and the woods for their green deliciousness.

So after the winter is over, we watch. And then the onions grow, the wild onions grow. And we go out and we harvest onions. They're like scallions. They have stalks with a bulb on the end. And they're very tasty, very good. We pick them every year. I've been picking them now for seventy years.

And after the onions grow, then we have leeks. They grow in the woods and you need a shovel to get them because they grow in clumps. We pick them and we cook them up.

One time Helen and I were digging leeks out in Earlville. And we didn't ask permission. There was this big field of leeks. We went out there and we were picking leeks, enjoying ourselves. It was just fun. And I had a big thirty-three gallon trash bag and it was three-quarters full. And a car came up to the corner and stopped. And this woman came out, a white-haired woman. And she was waving her hands and she was hollering, "You're on private property and who gave you permission?" and, you know, the whole bit.

I stood there and I watched and I waited until she got up to me. And she said, "You're on private property."

"Yeah," I said, "I realize that."

"What are you doing here?"

I said, "Well," I said, "I'm Chief Irving Powless Jr. from the Onondaga Nation. And every spring, we go out and we pick leeks. And leeks are like a tonic for us. And it's necessary for us to be out digging leeks and to enjoy the fruits of what . . . the gifts of the Creator."

"Well," she said, "you don't have my permission to do that, and you're on private property. Besides that," she said, "I have a whole bunch of wild-flowers here and I don't want my flowers ruined."

I said, "Well, lady," I said, "look in my bag." And I showed her this bag. I said, "You see all these leeks that I have in my bag?"

And she said, "Yes."

I said, "Tell me where I picked them from."

She said, "What?"

I said, "Tell me where I picked these from."

So she walked around her field. And she couldn't tell where I'd picked the leeks from. And I said, "You see all your flowers? They're still there," I said, "I didn't touch any of your flowers." I said, "I haven't even . . . ," I said, "You can't tell where I picked these things from."

And she looked around and she said, "That's right. Okay." She said, "You now have my permission to come here every year and pick leeks."

And I said, "Well, thank you ma'am." I said, "We appreciate that."

But it's the teachings of my dad that showed me how to do that. And so you can disrupt in a way that's not disruptive. And he had taught me that.

Then I was reading a book by historians, and I read the words, "You can't tell where these people have been. You don't know they've been there. You can't tell that they've been through here because they don't disrupt the environment."

And I thought, *Wow! Someone noticed a long time ago.* My dad didn't know that, but the teachings from his father, and from his grandfather, and so forth, had come down through history and they reached me. And so I passed this kind of information on to my boys, you know, that you have to know these things and to be aware of them.

Sad to say, some of the children that are living here at Onondaga today have not been into the woods. They have not been up and down the creeks. And they have not learned these things, you know, because only some of our people are hunting. So there's a change and we have to adapt to that. But we have to remember who we are and we have to remember these traditions.

And after the leeks, as spring turns to summer, the people again move to the fields, this time in search of berries. Strawberries are considered to be a special gift from the Creator, as he grew them so close to Mother Earth. So we give thanks to them also for continuing their duties. The Onondaga word for strawberries is *ohándadekhahgwih,* which translates to "field of fire."

And we're out in the fields picking the strawberries. And we thank the Creator for the strawberry that's still here. And every year we look forward to when they're coming so that we know that we'll be able to go out there and pick some. And make some sauce and maybe make some strawberry shortcake.

And after the strawberries, in July, come the blackberries. "Black caps" are what they're called, I guess, but we call them blackberries. And then, after the black caps, come the long blackberries. They're longer; they're not as sweet as the black caps. And they grow on a bush that is quite large. But we're out there picking those. And then that usually ends our summer harvesting: onions, dandelions, leeks, strawberries, blackberries, thimbleberries, and long blackberries.

And then in the fall, we're out picking butternuts, hickory nuts, pears, peaches, and apples. They all grow on the trees. And they're all mentioned in our Opening Address that we give. We give thanks to the trees that produce nuts and fruit. In the fall time, when they get ripe, we're out there picking them. So we're harvesting, all along, the gifts that the Creator has given to us. And every time we do that, we give thanks that they came back again.

And our gatherers are taught to take only what is needed. We learn not to deplete all of the resources and leave none for the people who are following us tomorrow. The lesson we are taught is to save for our grandchildren and for the people not yet born.

The Onondagas live in the beautiful Finger Lakes area of present-day New York. That allows us, for the spring and summer months, to fish in the abundant streams.

And a while back we went out and we went up to Otisco Lake in the springtime when the redfins were running. Redfins are about twenty-four inches long, they're about five or six inches around, and they're a delicious fish, you know. We had our burlap bag hung over my shoulder. And we went down to the lake and we were chasing fish all over that place. And, oh boy, that was fun. But when we got home with our big bag full of fish, we went around the community the next day. And we gave fish away. And people are still asking us, "When are you going to bring those fish to us again? Those fish were so delicious."

The fall and winter allowed for the hunting of deer, turkey, rabbit, and game found throughout the area. When hunters brought down a large game animal such as a deer, the hunters would take what they needed and distribute the rest to members of the community. This tradition still continues, and elders often are very excited and thankful when hunters return from a prosperous hunt. Our hunters are also taught to take only what is needed. The animals and the people live together on Mother Earth and it is important that everyone remains healthy to continue with their duties.

In the wintertime, we have a ceremony where we give thanks for all of these things. And we ask, hopefully, that we will be able to see them again. And every morning when we get up, we thank the Creator for the sun that came up, and we give thanks that we are here and we have seen the sun come up again. And we'll see the moon tonight. And hopefully, we'll see the sun tomorrow morning.

This is the way our life is, always giving thanks for everything that happens. We're not praying for things: we give thanks to the things that we have received. That's the difference between our two cultures.

Talking with your mouth "full"

I was watching a movie the other day. In the movie, this woman is talking to this man at breakfast time. And she has a plate of pancakes. She cuts the pancakes up into pieces and puts about one quarter of the pancake in her mouth and continues to chew and talk at the same time. And when she talks, you cannot tell that she's got a whole mouthful of food. Who are these people, anyway, that can do this? I certainly can't put food in my mouth and then talk as if I had nothing in my mouth.

Milkweed and roses

After the blackberries, we pick milkweed. And if you go out there and break them and taste the white stuff that's in them, milkweed are very bitter. But they have a nice flower, a red flower. And if you pick that red flower and make a batter up, run the flower through that, and then fry that, you have one nice meal.

And if you notice, if you have the time . . . you should have time anyway, I think, to smell the roses. Hectic as your life is, you have to stop, and smell the roses and the flowers. And enjoy the environment. And the milkweed is one of the things that we pick to eat. But it's not only a food for us, it's also a food for butterflies. The Monarch butterfly takes the nectar from the milkweed, and that's its food. So if you see milkweed, if you sit around—if you have the time—you'll see Monarch butterflies around them.

And it's very important to take the time to enjoy the environment.

I'll illustrate this: the other day I was sitting in my kitchen looking out the window. And there was a southern breeze blowing. And it was blowing so that the trees were bending towards the north. The leaves of the trees provided a canopy for the wind to move them. And as strong as the wind got, it was not time for the leaves to fall from the trees. So they hung on. And when the wind died down, each tree returned to its majestic stance, straight up in the air. It was fun to watch the trees as they moved back and forth with the gentle southern breeze that was coming through.

I also noticed that the way the wind was blowing, it was turning the leaves over, so you could see their undersides. And my father told me, when you see the underside of the leaves, you know it's going to rain.

And so I sat there, that day, and I said, *Oh, look at that. I see the underside of the leaves.*

And then the wind died down; the trees returned to their natural state. The branches of the trees returned to where they were before the wind blew. And the trees were standing there majestically the way they've always been, thirty feet high, overlooking Mother Earth, and doing what they're supposed to do.

Maybe those particular trees might be producing apples. But they take the time to sway with the breeze. To sit and to watch that was really something to see. I really enjoyed that. And then the next morning, guess what? I woke up to the thunder. Thunder was rolling across the sky. And I said, *What a wonderful sound!* And as I listened, I could hear the rain on the roof. I said, *Well, the trees told me yesterday that rain was coming. And here it is. I'm going to go out and watch.*

So I went out and I watched the rain.

And this is what you have to do. In your hectic life, you have to stop and enjoy the environment. Look at the trees: watch them as they move. Watch the plants. Watch the birds as they go from limb to limb and they sing their songs. Listen to their songs because they're singing them for you to enjoy. Watch the butterflies as they move around.

And if you've got time, you can sit and watch the grass grow! It's hard to see if you sit and watch. But if you go away and come back a week later, you can see that the grass is taller than it was, so you know that it grew. But to sit there and watch it grow, that's something else!

You should take the time to do that because it eases the tension and the stress from your hectic life. And all the time, when friends tell me how busy they are and what they're doing, I say, "Well, don't forget to stop to smell the roses and the flowers. Enjoy the environment, and enjoy what the Creator has given to us."

And so I suggest to you people that are reading, that you do the same thing. Take time tomorrow, to go out and enjoy the environment, the plants, the flowers, the birds, the butterflies, or whatever's out there, that you can see. And the winds that are blowing.

George Washington's empire

On a different subject, the *intent* of the 1794 Treaty with the United States was to give free passage through our territory. In 1783, George Washington publicly announced his genocide policy against Native Americans. He looked from the east shore of Lake Oneida, looked west, and said, "What a place to build an empire! I think I'll build an empire." But in order to build an empire, he had to get rid of the people who were living there.

Us. And all of the Natives west of us.

So a genocide policy was set in place at that time, to get rid of all of the Native people, so he could build his empire. Now this is unknown by most non-Native people—or if it's known, it's ignored—because they don't teach it in schools. I've talked to many college graduates about our history. When I tell them, they say, "We never heard of these things." They were not taught this in school, that there were treaties. They were not taught that there were treaty obligations on their part. And there are treaty obligations on our part that we still maintain and uphold. And in many cases we have never violated these treaties. But these treaties are continually violated every day by the United States and the state of New York.

So the federal government wanted to expand, but we were in the way. So they said, "Well, one way to expand is to get rid of them." So in 1779 they sent John Sullivan into our territory. And they destroyed our villages; they killed our women and children; they destroyed our food source, so that if we escaped their army, then we would starve to death—we would have no food.

Now that policy of genocide started in 1779 and continues on up 'til today. And everybody knows the name of that guy who attacked the

Lakotas: George Custer. That's all part of that, because he was out there to do the same thing, to eliminate Native Americans.

He didn't do a good job, according to the US Army, because he was defeated. And other army generals that came out also did the same thing. They were defeated by our people. But we are still under attack. We're still fighting to exist as a people.

So a couple of years ago we put in a land claim for a process to heal. A process to heal, because we have been subjected to a policy of genocide.

It's very important that you make sure we survive

And back to what I was talking about before, the Haudenosaunee are a spiritual people. We were talking to the EPA [the Environmental Protection Agency], which is only thirty years old. And we said to them that it's about time that you realize that you've got to protect the environment. You've been around for 200 years, and just thirty years ago you decided the environment needs to be protected?

We've been living this way all of our lives, thousands of years. And because of that we know how things work and why we have to have ceremonies. And so we were talking to the EPA and we were arguing and I said, "Well, you are against us. So if you are against us, you are against the environment. And if you're against the environment, the environment is going to come and you aren't going to be able to stop the environment."

It was shortly after that that Katrina hit New Orleans. And it went through New Orleans and it didn't stop. It went up the Mississippi River. And I talked to Janice Whitney of the EPA. I called her up and I told her, you know, I reminded her, that the winds were blowing again and that Katrina was going up the Mississippi. "Yeah," she said, "I heard." She said, "I'm in Rochester."

I said, "Well, watch where the winds go."

Well, what happened was, Katrina came up the Mississippi for a ways and then turned east and headed towards New York, the territory of the Haudenosaunee. It started that way, but then it stopped and turned north and headed north. It stayed north and it went in between Lake Erie and Lake Ontario. And it went up on the north side of Lake Ontario.

It never went into Haudenosaunee territory. And I had told Janice to check. So if you want, you know, you could check with her, to see if this actually happened. And hopefully she remembers that this is what happened, when that wind came up. It headed towards Haudenosaunee territory, but it stopped. And it went in between the two lakes and went up into Canada on the north side of Lake Ontario. And it never came into New York.

And that's because we *are* the environment. And we're not going to bring 100-mile-an-hour winds into our territory. I just say this as a reminder of who we are as spiritual people and how connected we are to the environment.

I heard on television one day that the ocean was our enemy. This is what the reporter said. And I said, "How can you say this?" The ocean is one of our best friends. Because without the ocean, we would not survive. Because the ocean provides so much for us, to sustain our life. And to call it an enemy is in total opposition to who we are and what we're about. Because the ocean is our friend, a very important friend.

When this reporter called the ocean an enemy, I said, "Well, no wonder they've got problems. They think the ocean is an enemy because they cannot control it. They're not going to be able to control the environment or the winds, the rains, the floods, the waters, and so forth. They can't control that. When it happens, it happens."

But we have ceremonies that keep things in order so that they happen the way they're supposed to happen, the way they've been happening for thousands of years. Because if we don't have these ceremonies, you won't have that continuity. So it's very important that you take care of us, and make sure that we survive. Because if we're gone—as I heard on TV again the other day—they said, "When the Indian stops giving, it's going to be a bad world, because the Indian gives us so much. He takes care of things. So it's necessary for us to have the Indian." This is what was on TV the other day.

But I add this to the book just for information or things I'm thinking that you should know about.

The women have a very strong place

There's a whole bunch of other differences in our politics that I could illustrate, you know. But if you look at our government and your government and what we presented in 1744 and what you did with it, they're two entirely different things. The women, see, for the last 2,000 years, for over 2,000 years, have had a very strong political place in our government.

When you wrote the Constitution, you left the women out. You didn't give them a vote. They weren't even counted in the census. And they fought for years to get recognition. And Susan B. Anthony and Matilda Joslyn Gage, who lived in Fayetteville, New York, came and talked with the Haudenosaunee women about their place in the political world of the Haudenosaunee. Their house still stands on Route 5 as you enter Fayetteville.

And from what they learned about our women, they said, "Well, we should work toward that." And so the women's suffrage movement came into being. And it was finally agreed, you know, that women would be able to vote. And they'd be counted and so forth. But that all came about because those women were talking to our women, about women in politics.

There's no one higher than the other

Which brings up another thought that's contrary to how we think. In our society we don't have a separation of class. When we sit in council, we are all the same. We all have equal power. And there's no one higher than the other. We sit there all at the same level. We all have the same duties; we all have the same responsibilities; we all have the same vote and the ability to discuss these issues.

And this is what we told Benjamin Franklin and those people in 1744. But for some reason or other, they didn't feel that that would be the way they would go. So they wrote the Constitution and they figured out a way to have people sit in the House of Representatives. And as I've already mentioned, article 2 of the Constitution says they will count the people to determine how many people will sit in the House of Representatives, excluding blacks, women, and Indians. So all men are *not* created equal by the Constitution of the United States. Blacks are not equal. Indians aren't and *women* are not equal.

But in our society, everybody's equal. And we don't have class distinctions.

You've got rich people; you've got poor people. Well, we have rich people and poor people, also, but at a function we're all together. That doesn't happen in your society. If the rich people have a function, only the rich people are there. The poor people aren't invited.

Or, for example, in high school you enter as a freshman. Freshman, then sophomore, then junior and senior—and these classes don't mix. Seniors don't mingle with the freshmen. When you have a senior dance, only seniors go. You have a freshman dance, only freshmen go there. The sophomores and juniors and seniors don't go or can't go or whatever. They're excluded.

When we have a dance, *everybody* goes. In the middle of the floor of the longhouse will be a bench on which the singers are sitting. And they will sing songs for the dance that we're doing: for the Fish, Raccoon, Duck, or whatever. Whatever dance—Moccasins, Women's Dance. . . . And so, on the bench is the lead singer and everyone else helps him out. There will be mostly men, but there might also be a teenager or a ten-year-old sitting on the bench. And your society would not allow that to happen, but it is allowed in our society. Because we're all equal.

And that boy that's sitting on the bench, he doesn't know the songs. But he's learning. And one day he will be sitting there with the drum, singing. And there will be another younger one sitting there, learning.

And it's so clear to me, you know, to see this difference from our society, as to how you treat each other. A very distinct division between one class of people and another class. And we don't have that.

If we have a function, *everybody* goes.

We had a lacrosse game, a medicine game, and I was one of the players for one of the teams. I was seventy-one years old at the time that this game was going on. There were teenagers playing in this game. And I wasn't the oldest one on the floor. There was this guy there that was eighty years old playing in this game. So we've got teenagers and eighty-year-olds all playing in the same game. Unheard of in your society to have such a mixture.

He struck a match and the water coming out of the faucet was on fire!

Now another example of why you have to look at the effects of all of these things you do in the natural world: hydrofracking. This is a process used when companies are looking for gas. And in order to get at the gas, they have to go down into the earth. They drill a hole down. And then once they get down into the hole, they turn at a 90-degree angle and they drill horizontally. And I don't know how far they go, but they go quite a ways.

A couple of weeks ago [in January 2010] they had an article in the paper about this fellow down in Binghamton. They showed him turning the water faucet on. He struck a match, and the water coming out of the faucet was on fire! And that's a result of this hydrofracking in Pennsylvania south of Binghamton.

This is clearly a violation of the treaty that we made with the people from the Netherlands in the early 1600s. I don't know how we stop it because we've talked to the EPA. There was a ban on this kind of drilling in the New York City watershed. I asked them about the rest of the state. And they said, "Well, the DEC does that." They have no control over what the DEC does. And the DEC has the power to give permits out for these people to drill. If they drill and they contaminate our water, then we're not going to have any water here at Onondaga, you know.

And right now we can go up to Gibson Road with a cup and drink the water that's coming right out of the earth. And there aren't too many places you can do that today. But here on Onondaga Territory, we have a couple of places like that, where we can go with a cup and dip our water directly out of Mother Earth. You can see the water coming right out of the earth.

And there are places like Little Falls, where you can stick your cup in there and get it full of water. And drink that. It's nice, cold, clear water—clean, nice-tasting. And to have the DEC issue a permit to some company to go in there and pollute our water is a violation of the treaty. So this is just a reminder that we have to do what we can to preserve the water for tomorrow.

Because right now we've got a three-million-dollar water system here where everybody on the reserve doesn't have to worry about the wells being polluted from the salt—the process of brine lines that run through the territory. And our water is nice and clear, clean and fresh—no chemicals. It's nice, clean, clear water. And we have to keep it that way, if we can.

So how are we going to do that? There was an article in a magazine called *Waterkeeper* on hydrofracking. And it shows a picture of the drilling, the same kind of drilling that Pennsylvania is doing. And the article talks about what they do and the chemicals they put in there. But it doesn't tell us that they are polluting wells. And this is what we have to stop, if we can.

The songs that were given to us so long ago are still being carried on today

The Onondaga ceremonies give thanks and reflect the surrounding living world. Dances and songs are performed in a counterclockwise direction. The bean plant, Mother Earth, the moon, and the stars—they all move in this life-providing direction. And so do we when we dance. In this fashion, the songs that were given to us so long ago are still being carried on today.

Our songs are sung using drums and rattles. Drums are usually made of cedar trees with deer hide stretched over the top. A small portion of a cedar log is hollowed out and waterproofed. Water is then poured into the bottom of the drum and the deer hide is stretched over the top of the cedar. The wet leather is then stretched and tightened before playing, for a nice tone.

The Onondaga and Haudenosaunee generally use two types of rattles. The horn rattle usually accompanies the water drum. The horn rattle is an animal horn, which also has been hollowed out. Then seeds are placed inside and a wooden top, bottom, and handle are added. These rattles are used by the singers who accompany the lead singer. The lead singer plays the water drum.

The second type of rattle is the turtle rattle. This rattle is very sacred to the Haudenosaunee and is only used in a few select ceremonies. A snapping turtle is caught for the sole purpose of making this special rattle. Once the turtle has been sacrificed and hung to dry, skilled craftsmen carve wooden braces that are braced inside the shell along with seeds, before the rattle is sewn back together. An individual who owns such a rattle takes great care in preserving it because a turtle's life was sacrificed for the ceremonies it now participates in.

But we don't just dance in our ceremonies, we also dance in the evening at our socials.

What a sad situation in the white man's world!

The other day I was listening to the radio, and this girl came on and sang a song about dancing with her father when she was a little girl. And now that she's a grown woman, she wishes she could dance with her father again.

And I said to myself, *Boy, how sad. What a sad situation in the white man's world!* Because I danced with my father when I was a little boy. And I danced with him when I was a teenager: I was a fifteen-year-old at the time, and he was forty. And for the next thirty-five years, my father and I danced together. The last time I danced with him, he was seventy-five years old.

So there's a big difference between your society and my society in that I've danced with my sons for most of their lives. My oldest son is something like fifty-three years old; I've been dancing with him for fifty-three years. My second son is thirty-eight; I've been dancing with him for thirty-eight years. And so we're still dancing, still dancing yet. I'm eighty years old and we still dance together.

So how sad in the white man's world that this doesn't usually happen between parents and their children: they don't dance together. But in our society this happens all the time. We have a dance: everybody dances. We've got children dancing that are three years old, four years old; we've got eighty-year-olds up there dancing together. So it's quite likely that there are other families—besides myself, you know—that have danced with their parents for thirty, forty, fifty, sixty years, depending upon their age and how long they last.

So we don't have a distinction between our age groups. That does not happen in your society, that I know of. But it does happen in our society.

When we have a social, our young children participate in every aspect of it: they're spectators, they're singers, they're dancers. And your society does not seem to ever do that. You go to see something, you are only one of these: either you are a spectator or you are a performer or a musician. But you don't change in the middle of the ceremony and become one of the other ones.

But we do this all the time. We go to a social and we sit as spectators. And the one who is organizing it will come to the people who are sitting and pick ones to be the singers and ones to be the dancers. So you come as a spectator, but you end up being one of the performers.

And so this is how it is that we are able to dance with our parents all our lives. I've danced with my kids all their lives. My daughter, she'll be fifty-six. I've been dancing with her for fifty-six years. And I will continue dancing with her because I'm only eighty. So I'll be dancing a while yet. And her being fifty-five—she's real active and a good dancer. And so she'll be dancing for a while. And she's dancing with her daughter, who's twenty-six. So they're both young, and they've got years of dancing together ahead of them. And my grandson is six. His father is only thirty-eight, so they will be dancing together for a long time.

Not like this girl who was thinking she danced with her father when she was a little girl and now she wishes she could dance with him again. It's not a wish in our society: we do this all the time.

And we will live alongside you;
we will coexist

It is important to realize the concept of what was put to the people who were coming into our territory in the early 1600s. We said to you, "You come into our territory; you live here under *our* laws." And our laws say that we will respect each other. Now, we don't know who you are: we don't speak the same language, you have a different government, you have different leaders, and you have different laws. You have a different religion. And we respect that. And you can live in our territory with those concepts.

And we will live alongside you. We will coexist, and you will have the same respect for us, for our differences, our different government, our different ways, religion—if you want to call it that. But you have to have respect. And I don't see that in your society. You don't seem to have respect. The seniors don't have respect for the freshmen. They will not allow them to come to their functions because they're lower than, they're not equal to. . . .

But our society welcomes everybody. Everybody can be part of. . . . And so when we have a function, everybody shows up: rich people, poor people, tall people, short people, thin people, fat people. And we're all equal. And we all respect the other ones for who they are and what they contribute to the community.

One of these days, hopefully, you will be able to realize what was said in the early 1600s when we met. And agree to coexist in our territory on Mother Earth. And you will have respect not only for yourselves and your fellow people, but also for us. We're still functioning under your 1600 concepts of "savages" and *not equal*. And though we have contributed to

113

and made your government what it is today—because of the knowledge that we gave to you—we are still looked down on as being Indians and not capable of formulating something that would be beneficial.

But it was Benjamin Franklin who said, "These savages that we're talking to have been able to form a government that has existed for a long time. They've joined five nations together. And as a people who are moving into their territory, we would find it beneficial if we could join our people together and form a union such as theirs. It would be very advantageous for us to do that." And so this finally did happen. You joined your thirteen colonies together and started your United States. And now you have grown into fifty states. But it appears that you still don't have the respect that you should have, the respect you need in order to function as a community for the benefit of all of your people and for the benefit of all of the people of the world.

Renewing our peace and friendship . . . and our obligations

The Canandaigua Treaty of November 11, 1794, is a continuation of the Two Row Wampum Belt commemorating the treaty made in the early 1600s. And in the Two Row we said, "In the future we will meet. And when we meet, we will renew our obligations to each other."

So the Canandaigua Treaty is a renewal of our obligations to each other. That's why article 1 stresses the meeting is for peace and friendship. Because that was the basis for the Two Row—that we would co-exist together in peace and friendship. Forever. And whenever we meet in the future, we would renew our obligations to each other.

So this is what the Canandaigua Treaty is. What was written about the Canandaigua Treaty is written on two pages. It only contains about a page and a half of literature. But the intent of the treaty is not there. The intent of the treaty is to continue the friendship established in the Two Row.

And the United States was looking to expand. And in order to expand, they had to go out west. And to go west, they had to go through our territory. So the Canandaigua Treaty was a meeting for them to sit down and discuss how they would be able to travel through our territory.

They said to us that they wanted to travel through our territory to get out west. And in order to do so, they would build roads. They would build the roads, they would maintain them, and there would be no cost to us for these roads. And we would never have to pay a toll on any one of the roads.

This treaty was completely ignored by the state when they built the New York State Thruway. Because the thruway charges people that travel on the road, and that includes us. So we're paying a toll on a road that violates the Canandaigua Treaty. Because they said at that time we would be able to travel the roads without paying any toll.

Of course this is a New York State highway. And if New York State was paying attention to the treaties, they could have had the federal government build that road at no cost to the state—just like Route 81, which goes through the State of New York. It's a federal highway—and it didn't cost the state anything—to get from Canada to Pennsylvania. And the road didn't cost us anything either.

But the *intent* of the treaty is for them to have free passage through our territory. This is still that way today. They travel the road, that Route 81. And the *intent* is that we should be able to travel that road also at no cost to us. So this is primarily what the Canandaigua Treaty was about: renewing the friendship—the existing peace and friendship—forever. And free passage through our territory.

And it was at this treaty that Timothy Pickering stated that he was negotiating "so that the chain of friendship would be brightened."

Part of taking care of Mother Earth is doing ceremonies and giving thanks

The Creator gave us a way of life. It is important that we remember our duties as Onondaga people. One of our duties is to take care of Mother Earth. Part of taking care of Mother Earth is doing ceremonies and giving thanks to the Creator and all of creation for still performing their duties.

The people responsible for ensuring that our ceremonies are still being performed hold a great responsibility in the community. These men and women are commonly called "faithkeepers." These people refer to the seasons and the lunar calendar to decide when our ceremonies are to take place.

There are many ceremonies that take place throughout the year. Our first ceremony to begin the new (lunar) year is called Midwinter. Midwinter lasts for twenty-one days. Each day of Midwinter we are giving thanks for many different things and performing different ceremonies. Midwinter provides a great feeling of harmony with the Creator and celebrates our time together on Mother Earth.

Listed below are some of the ceremonies given to us by the Creator that are still being conducted in the longhouse today:

Midwinter Ceremony
Maple Sap Ceremony
Planting Ceremony
Bean Ceremony
Strawberry Ceremony
Green Corn Ceremony
Harvest Ceremony

The faithkeepers, who are responsible for initiating when these ceremonies begin, rely on the lunar calendar. Below are the names of the moons and the translation of each.

Onondaga	English
Hisatuh	Treacherous little winter
Ganahdoha	Leaf buds are on the leaves
Ganahdogo:nah	Moon of many leaves
Ohiaihah	Little ripening of the berries
Ohiaihgo:nah	Great ripening of the berries
Saskeh hah	Long daylight
Saskehgo:nah	Big, long daylight
Kendenhah	Deer has a short tail
Kendenhgo:nah	Deer has a long tail
Jotowehhah	Return of the little cold
Jotowego:nah	Return of the big cold
Disuh	Long nights, short days
Disgo:nah	Longer nights, shorter days

The preservation of our way of life and of ourselves as a people is most important. We are the ones who are speaking for the species of life. And that's the fish in the water, the birds in the trees, the plants, the thunder, the rain—and the treaties that help to protect them. All of these elements are part of us. The ceremonies that we do take care of the harmony between those elements and us as a people. And the preservation of that is so *important*.

And it's not just the Haudenosaunee. It's all of the Indigenous people of the United States and Alaska and Canada, and Central and South America. All the Indigenous peoples have the same message, the same concept, the same idea between themselves and the environment and the preservation of the environment.

We were there

One of the things that happens when I meet with dignitaries from the state or the federal government is that I usually talk about history, the treaties, and so forth. I do that so that they will have a better understanding as to why I make certain statements and the meanings behind them. My statements are based on treaties and commitments and obligations that were made 200 years ago.

So I will say, "Well, when we were at Fort Stanwix . . . ," or, "When we were at Canandaigua, this is what we said and this is what we decided." And I talk this way because when I tell our oral history, the people who told me this said it that way: "When we were here, this is what was said."

And so when I repeat the story, I say it the way it was told to me. For example, "When we were at Fort Stanwix, this is what was said. At the Treaty of Canandaigua in 1794, the intent of the treaty was for the United States to have free passage through our territory. So they wanted to build roads. And they said that they would build roads; they would maintain them. And it would be at no cost to us: that we would never have to pay a toll."

And so, if we look at the Canandaigua Treaty as it was written, there is a sentence in there that refers to a toll road to Buffalo. And it says *in* the treaty that the Natives don't have to pay a toll on that road. So the intent of the treaty is there. So when I'm telling people from the state or the federal government about the treaty—because they've never read it—I say, "When we were at Canandaigua in 1794, this is what we said."

And they look at me and say to themselves, *How old is this guy anyway? That was in 1794. That's over 200 years ago, and he was there?*

I say, you know, "But this is the way we talk." And so people think that because I talked that way that I was at this treaty. And *spiritually* I was there because someone was there with my name. Dehatgahdoñs was there at that meeting. And that's my name. Dehatgahdoñs was there, so I have no problem with saying I was there.

But what works in your community doesn't necessarily work in our community, or vice versa. There is a conflict of understandings of how that is.

I mentioned before that I had been with my father in the woods from the time I was a teenager. So from 1945, when I was fifteen or sixteen years old, until he passed away in 1985 I spent forty years with this man. And during this time he told me a lot of stories about how it was when he was growing up. The stories that he told me are what I use to explain how it used to be here, and what's not here, and what we've lost environmentally in the line of animals and so forth, vegetables, fruits, and stuff. So there's been a big change environmentally. And with the animal world, what used to be here is not here anymore.

So when I tell these things, I say, "This is how it was. And the Two Row Wampum Treaty says we will make sure that what's here today will be here for future generations." So my father told me how it used to be. And I say, "Well, in his generation that's what he saw. I have never seen that." So people are violating that treaty because what he saw, I've never seen. And it's not because of something that we've done—it's something the outside world has done. What used to be here is not here anymore. So it's important for us to realize that these treaties that we had . . . and I wasn't there in the early 1600s, but this is what we said at that time: "We will allow you to come and live in our territory, as long as you live by the natural laws."

And they said, "Well, we can do that. But what are the natural laws?"

The natural laws are that you will maintain and keep what's here today for future generations. If there are deer, rabbits, raccoons, and pheasants here at this time, your great-grandchildren will be able to hunt these animals because we will have protected them for future generations.

And that's what was said. And we agreed upon it at that time. We also agreed that we would refer to each other as brothers. So when I refer to you, today, I refer to you as brother. Because that's what we agreed upon in the early 1600s.

Haudenosaunee humor 2

But our lifestyles are different. And what your people do is sometimes not understood or accepted by us. For example, I was in the woods one day with my dad. And he said, "You know, the white people have a way of seeking help when they're in the woods. They fire three shots in the air. And that means that they're in distress. People will go to where the shots come from and will help them out." He said, "And I'm not too sure about where we are, so maybe you'd better fire three shots. And we'll get some assistance."

I said, "All right." So I got up and I walked about five or ten yards away from him. And I fired three shots in the air. And I came back and sat down with him. And we sat there for an *hour* and nobody came to help us.

So my dad said to me, "Gee, that's odd. They didn't come to see what was wrong or if we needed help or anything." He said, "You'd better go fire three more shots in the air."

And I said, "I can't."

He said, "You can't?"

I said, "No, I'm out of arrows."

You will know who we are by the way we are dressed

Back in the 1960s, there seemed to be an identity crisis, not only in the United States but in Indian Country. People were walking around calling themselves flower children, hippies, whatever. There was a move to identify themselves with who they wanted to be or what they wanted to be—not necessarily as US citizens, but as people belonging to a group that they could identify with.

We kind of went through something like that, too. Because up until that time, whenever we went out we presented ourselves the way people expected us to be. So we wore our leggings, moccasins, armbands, necklaces, and headdress. But we were bare from the waist up because that's how they expected Indians to be. So that's the way we were.

Because of the movies that were out in the 1950s and '60s—mostly about the West and about the Lakotas with their big thirty-two-feathered war bonnets—they expected us to be like that. So we were wearing Lakota headdresses when we went out. Bare-chested, but Lakota headdress on.

But we have our own headdress. It's called a *gustoweh*. It's the most distinctive feature of our Haudenosaunee men's dress. It's a fitted hat, like a cap, made out of strips of wood with a cloth covering, with stripped feathers: eagle, hawk, pheasant, or turkey feathers. The gustoweh is also used to identify an individual's nation. A man wearing his gustoweh with one feather pointing straight up in the air and another feather hanging in the back, pointing downwards, indicates he is Onondaga. So one feather up and one feather down is Onondaga. Two up and one down is Oneida. Three up is Mohawk. One down is Cayuga. A man who has one feather pointing skyward is identified as Seneca. None—no feathers—is

Tuscarora. Each nation has their own way of identifying each other by their gustoweh. So when we meet and we all have our headdresses on, you can tell what nation we belong to by our hats.

Anyway, all this came about in about 1972. We started wearing shirts instead of going out bare-chested; we took off our Lakota headdresses and started wearing our own. And we identified ourselves as who we were, not what the people expected us to be.

The Onondaga people and the rest of the nations of the Haudenosaunee, we have our own style. Since we are woodland people, we dress different than Native peoples who reside in the plains. Feathers that cascade away from a person's body are indeed well-suited for the open plains, but not for carving your way through wooded paths.

Long ago, the Onondagas relied on the animals to provide clothing. The deer was obviously a great source for food and clothing. All parts of the deer were utilized. The brain was used to help cure and tan the hide. The hide was used for dresses, leggings, moccasins, aprons, and wraps. Sinew from the deer was used for sewing and for making bows. The bone of the deer was used to make knives, arrowheads, and elaborate combs.

After contact with our white brothers, we began to adapt their clothing materials to our style of clothing. Beads made from clam shells were gradually replaced by glass. Sinew was replaced by cotton thread. The women wore loose-fitting blouses, often decorated with a beaded yoke. Woolen skirts and leggings now began to be decorated with beadwork. But nothing has replaced the feel of deerskin moccasins lined with rabbit fur!

The men have gone through similar changes in dress. Leggings, once solely made of deer, are at times made with wool. And the transition to men always wearing decorative shirts is relatively new to our area. In fact when the Tuscaroras first joined the Haudenosaunee in the late 1700s, they were identified as the "Shirt Wearers."

And way back in the early 1600s, in the treaty between the people from the Netherlands and the Haudenosaunee, we had told them, "So, from this day forward we will know each other as brothers. And in the future when we meet, you will know who we are by the way we are dressed and the way that we speak." Presenting ourselves as who we are also goes along with a statement that Geronimo made one day when he said, "I would rather present myself as who I am, rather than something that they want me to be."

And we expected that to mean that we would wear our leggings, our buckskins, our headdresses, our beadwork, and so forth. And through this we would identify ourselves as being Onondagas, Mohawks—Haudenosaunee—to the people that we meet socially and politically.

That is until one day I was sitting there listening to the radio and it said this person came into court "dressed in the laws of the state." And I said, "Wait a minute. That presents two ways of being dressed. One, we could appear at a meeting dressed in our clothes. But if we were dressed in American federal and state laws, we'd present a different person than the Haudenosaunee."

So today and every time that I have been out to meet with the dignitaries from the state or the federal government, I always dress so that they know who I am. I talked with Thomas Banyacya in the Hopi Nation and he said he does the same thing. Whenever he goes out, he wears clothes that identify him as a Hopi. He said, "That's what I am. And so when I go out, I greet people as a Hopi."

So that's what I do. And so I have my ribbon shirt on. And I have a bolo that I designed. It was made by a Native from Connecticut; he's a very good silversmith. And this is the only one in the world. It's about three sheets of silver; it's real heavy and the silversmith who made this brooch for me told me it was worth $3,000!

And I told him after he did it, "Well, you have my permission to use this design and make others for the other Haudenosaunee nations." Because what this does is it represents the Onondagas. There are fourteen chiefs in Onondaga. I'm one of them. So I have fourteen figures around the center. Our wampum belts that we use for identification and for recording events, they're made out of quahog shell from the coast. And that's what's in the center of this brooch. And I belong to the Wolf Clan, so there's the head of a wolf on here.

I told the person that made the brooch for me, I said, "You could use this for anybody from any of our nations who wants something similar to this. Like the Mohawks have got nine leaders—they could put nine figures around instead of fourteen. They would have a brooch that represents the Mohawk Nation and their nine leaders."

And he said, "No, I made one. I'm not going to make any more." He said, "I broke all my tools making this!" So I have the only one in the world like that.

But anyway, so in the early 1600s we sat down and decided we would call each other brothers. We decided that in the future when we meet, we will address each other as brothers. And we decided that they will know who we are by the way we are dressed. So that not only means by the clothes that we wear, but it has a legal meaning.

So you can see by the clothes I am wearing that I stand here before you as a citizen of the Onondaga Nation, a citizen of the Haudenosaunee—not as a citizen of the United States. If I come to you as a citizen of the United States, I've changed my status. So I come dressed in the laws and the traditions of the Onondagas and the Haudenosaunee, not the laws and the traditions of your government. I'm different. I have different status. I have different laws and I have treaties.

So ever since I heard that statement, every time I walk into court I present Onondaga laws, Haudenosaunee laws or customs. And I present myself as Onondaga or Haudenosaunee. So the court has no problem identifying who I am and that my laws are different than what's being presented in the court. And therefore the court doesn't have jurisdiction. It can't rule against us.

And so far, because of this presentation, I have won in the court cases I talked about earlier, a number of times. Those two decisions that I mentioned still stand.

So, it is very important to us to present ourselves as we said we would do in the early 1600s. "You will know who I am by the way I am dressed." And when I present that, I will be literally dressed in my Native dress, but legally I will present it in the laws and customs of the Onondagas and the Haudenosaunee. They are two different ways of presenting yourself.

The people in Massachusetts didn't realize this. And they put a court case in on land claims. And the judge said to them, "When is the last time you had a ceremony? Let me hear you speak your language." And the ones who were presenting the case couldn't do that. And so the judge ruled that they were not Wampanoags, but they were "descendants of Wampanoags." Therefore they had no case and their case was dismissed.

So after that decision and after what I heard on the radio, I make sure that I present myself both ways—in clothes and legally—as Onondaga or Haudenosaunee. That's very important not only for me, but for all that are coming in the future, to understand that this is how they must present themselves. And that way there's no question as to who you are. And there's no question when you quote from the Two Row that says we will not pass any laws telling you what you can do and what you can't do. And you, on the other hand, will not pass laws against us.

So when you present yourselves that way and you start looking at the laws that the federal government has passed, in U.S.C. [United States Code] Title 25—it's a federal book, Indian Law 25—you look at all of those laws, and all those laws are in violation of the Two Row. New York State McKinney book 25 is full of New York State laws that also violate the treaties.[*]

So it's very important for our people who are coming in or are learning about themselves to be able to identify themselves as such, that they are Onondagas and Haudenosaunee. And they will dress that way, politically and legally. And so the words of Geronimo were very prophetic when he said, "I would rather present myself as who I am, rather than something that they want me to be."

---

[*] *McKinney's Consolidated Laws of New York Annotated*, "Indian Law," book 25 (Eagan, MN: Thomson Reuters/West, 2011).

The difference between the laws, the conflict

I've just been talking about our laws and being dressed in our laws when I make a presentation. What I haven't talked about is the difference between the laws, the conflict. So I'd like to add this.

Our laws conflict. When the federal government passed [the laws codified in] 25 U.S.C. 232 and 233, which give New York State criminal and civil jurisdiction, they put a passage in the law that says that we have the right to hunt and fish without a license, based on treaties and customs. Now, "customs" means it's not in your laws. For instance, your law says you can hunt deer from December 3rd until March 5th, or something like that. Any time after that—you're illegal if you shoot a deer.

But my custom says, if I need a deer, I go out and hunt. And I shoot a deer. And if I do it in your territory outside of your laws and so forth, I'll get arrested. But if you arrest me, you're violating that law 25 (because federal law [U.S.C. title] 25 says I can hunt in your territory without a license, following my customs).

For instance, I get sick and I need a ceremony to cure my sickness. And the food for that ceremony is a deer. And it happens to be in March or April. So I have to go out and shoot a deer for that ceremony. And that's following my customs. But it's a violation of the laws that you have in place. And so our laws conflict with each other.

And there are other instances. Because depending upon the ceremony, I might need a bear or I might need a rabbit or I might need a pheasant or a fish. Some of the foods that we need are not in our territory anymore and they're very scarce in your territory. But I do go to your territory and I know where they are.

And if I go out there and I have to be in someone's yard gathering plants, they say, "Well, you're trespassing."

And I say, "No, I have the right. I have the right to do this." By your laws I don't have the right to do this, but with my customs, that say if this is what I need to do . . . then I'm following my custom.

So you say I'm violating your law. And I say, "I have treaty rights to hunt, to fish, and to gather according to my customs in your territory."

In our territory, we don't have fences, so we can travel anywhere in our territory. And in your territory, you have fences and you have signs saying "no trespassing," which means you can't go into that territory without having permission. We don't have such laws in our territory. If I need to get wild onions, for instance, I just go and pick them no matter where they are. And sometimes I'm on someone's property, but nothing is ever said about me picking onions on their property.

But if *you* go where there's a sign up that says "no trespassing," and you cross that fence without permission, you get arrested for trespassing. So our laws are very different in this sense.

This is important. It is important to know that we have the right by treaty to do this. We have fishing and gathering rights, starting with the treaty made in the early 1600s with the Dutch and with the first treaty that we made with England after that, in 1664. On September 24, 1664, Haudenosaunee representatives met in Albany with Colonel George Cartwright. The 1664 treaty included the provision "that they may have free trade, as formerly" (that is, as previously under the Dutch).

So we have maintained all of these times—every time we sat down and polished the chain of friendship, and we renewed our treaty obligations—we have reminded you that we have the right to do these things based on the Two Row. And we still maintain that this is the way it is.

And you can't pass a law that stops me from doing that because it's a violation of the treaty. And in order to change the treaty, you have to have both parties sitting there. This means you've got to have England and the Haudenosaunee sitting down together and reviewing this aspect of the treaty and agreeing to change it. Because if both are not in agreement, then it's not changed.

So this is a very important aspect of the law to understand.

Empty rooms

Haudenosaunee means "people of the longhouse." To us, our house is what is now the state of New York, with the Mohawks on the east end of our house. And the next part of the house is the Oneidas'. In the center, where the fire is, are the Onondagas. And then going further west are the Cayugas. And the Western Doorkeepers of the Haudenosaunee are the Senecas.

So living in this big state, we don't have enough people to cover all of it, just like you don't have enough people to cover the whole state. So you've got empty lots that could be called empty rooms. Because we didn't occupy everything, every space or every parcel, the Europeans that came into our territory would see an empty parcel. They would stop; they would build a home. Someone else would stop; they would build a home. Then they'd build a church, then they'd build a store. And then they would write to Albany and say, "We stopped here and we've established a town or a village. And we're calling it Earlville. Is that all right?"

They would send a letter to the capital. And Albany would write back and say, "Yes, that's all right. You can do that. And from here on out you will be known as the town of Earlville."

So I presented this at Colgate University when I was lecturing there on the Oneida land claims. And it's published in a book, *Iroquois Land Claims*.[*] Chris Vecsey published the book. And during the break in my presentation, we went to lunch. And when I came back, I passed a house. And in the house I looked into there was a TV, a chair, and a couch.

---

[*] Christopher Vecsey and William Starna, eds., *Iroquois Land Claims* (Syracuse, NY: Syracuse University Press, 1988).

And I said, "Oh, what a nice place to live. Maybe I should move in there." When I got back I was still the speaker, so I mentioned what had happened and my thoughts, that I should do this. I said, " . . . move into this house, into this empty room, and write to Onondaga and tell them I found this empty room and say, 'Is it all right if I live there?'"

Onondaga Nation would say, "Yes, you can live there."

And just as soon as I moved in, a whole bunch of people would show up to evict me from that empty room because it was in a part of a house. And I said, "Well, that's what you people did to us. You moved into our empty rooms. And all I'm doing is the same thing that you did."

And when I presented this, Alan van Gestel, the lawyer for the white people who were opposing the Oneida land claims, gave me a thumbs up, saying, you know, "You're right." Or, you know, "That's the conflict of laws." That was all right for the Europeans to do, to move into rooms in our empty house. But it's not okay for me to move into an empty room in a home that's owned by somebody, or owned by a corporation or whatever. Conflict of laws.

And when they moved into our territory and into our empty rooms, we defended our house. Today, New York State has a law that says if someone breaks into your house, you can shoot that person and you will not be charged for murder. But that law did not exist when the Europeans were moving into our empty rooms. So we were protecting our house just like the New York State law now states. But instead of saying "they're protecting their house," the Europeans called us hostiles and came after us and killed us for protecting our property.

So conflicting laws like this exist, not only in hunting and fishing, as I had mentioned before, but in protecting your own property. And I don't suppose we will be able to change what happened, but this is how we lost a lot of our territory. Because people moved into our empty rooms in our house.

And Haudenosaunee means "people of the longhouse." And our house was what is now the state of New York. And our rooms are occupied on the east by the Mohawks. Then the Oneidas. In the center of the state, where the fire of the Haudenosaunee is, live the Onondagas. And west of them are the Cayugas. And west of them are the Senecas. So those are the nations that live in the rooms of the longhouse. But we didn't occupy all of the rooms. And consequently the Europeans moved into our empty rooms and claimed them to be theirs.

Use of wampum

Now let's turn to another subject, a subject that the movie industry has confused people about: wampum. Wampum is made of white or purple shell—white from whelk shells and purple from quahog shells. They are shaped like small tubes or cylinders. They have holes drilled through them so that they can be strung as separate strings, strung in a circle, or woven into belts. These beads are living, spiritual. The shell is thought of as a living record.

The speaker puts the words of the agreement into the wampum. Each speaker thereafter uses the wampum to remember the initial agreement and the history that has happened to date.

Wampum has many uses and money is not one of them. Wampum is used to denote positions and record events and messages. One of the uses is to invite the other Haudenosaunee nations to meetings. These wampum strings are given [by runners to the other nations to indicate] the topic of the meeting—the topic that all of the nations are to meet and discuss. At the end of the wampum string is a wooden stick. The wooden stick tells the people of the nation when the meeting is to take place. As each day passes, a notch is cut off the stick. And when the notches are all gone, the meeting will take place.

Another use, for example, is that each leader has a wampum string that shows he holds a position among the Haudenosaunee. When a leader falls, the wampum is passed on to the new leader.

When a string of wampum is held in a person's hand, that person is said to be speaking truthfully. During ceremonies, the wampum strings are used to convey that the speaker's words are true. People listening to a speaker holding the wampum also know this and are very attentive and respectful of the speaker's message.

And the wampum belts are our history. For example, the Hiawatha Belt explains the union of the Mohawks, Oneidas, the Onondagas, the Cayugas, and Senecas. They formed together to make a union that we call the Haudenosaunee, the People of the Longhouse. Because our house is across the state of New York—containing the Mohawks, Oneidas, Onondagas, Cayugas, and Senecas—our house is big; it's a long house. That's why we're called the People of the Longhouse. And we lived in longhouses. Our houses were long and they had a lot of people in them.

When we joined together as one, we were spread across the state. So we named ourselves the Haudenosaunee, the People of the Longhouse, with the Senecas the Keepers of the Western Door. And the Onondagas are the Firekeepers because we are in the center. So it was set up that way, 2,000 years ago, and it's still that way today. We are still the Firekeepers. We Onondagas are also the Wampum Keepers—the wampum belts are here. The Senecas are still the Keepers of the Western Door. And the government that was set up 2,000 years ago is still here today.

The names of the leaders that were given are still here today. There were nine Mohawks, nine Oneidas, fourteen Onondagas, ten Cayugas, and eight Senecas. In total, fifty leaders for the Haudenosaunee. And then the names that were given at that time are still here today. I carry the name of Dehatgahdoñs, leader of the Beaver Clan for the Onondagas. I am the twenty-first name given, of the fifty—the third Onondaga name.

The names are still here, sitting with Thadodaho². Honoñwiyehdih sits on one side of him and Dehatgahdoñs on the other side. And the names that were put in the well are still there today. Bitter Throat still sits there. On the other side is Hahi·hoñh. We still sit in the same places that we were set in 2,000 years ago. So we are alive and well, and functioning as we were when we first formed together.

We are the longest existing government in the world. There is no other government that existed 2,000 years ago that operates the same way that they did 2,000 years ago like we do. Quite a statement.

Now the wampum belts also record the treaties. You have the Fort Stanwix Belt, the Canandaigua Belt . . . and how the Canandaigua Belt came to us and what the belt means. And what the treaty contains is not *written*. When we sat down to make the Treaty of Canandaigua in 1794, we started in July. And we sat in July, August, September, October, and then we signed in November. And if you read about the Canandaigua Treaty, it's on two pages—probably about a page and a half.

And there's no way that a page and a half of written language can contain the dialogue that went from July to November and what the intent of that treaty was. *But it's in our belts.*

So wampum is very important to the Onondaga and the Haudenosaunee. Therefore when the wampum belts left the community through the efforts of anthropologists, the Onondaga Nation worked diligently to have the wampum returned. In 1989 some belts returned after the determined efforts of the chiefs to bring these belts back to the people.

And because of a federal law called "NAGPRA" [Native American Graves Protection and Repatriation Act], which was passed in November 1990, all federally funded museums were told to return culturally affiliated objects. Because of this act, I was traveling around to various museums and I found flutes. And I thought just the western people played flute. So I asked the museum people what nation the flutes belonged to. And they said the Iroquois. So I made a flute and I taught myself how to play it. So I can sing an Onondaga song and I can also play the song on my flute.

I went to many museums where Native artifacts were held. But let's go back to the time when we got the belts back, and I'll tell you what happened. . . .

Repatriation of the wampum belts— a day that would not be forgotten

In order to tell the whole story, we have to go back to the late 1800s. And the reason I'm telling this is 'cause I don't recall—when I was telling about the belts on the nation's website—that I told this part. And this should be part of what is written about the return.

So anyway, right around 1890, we had a reverend here, Reverend William Beauchamp, who found out about the belts. And he wanted to know more about them. And he was talking to the person who was keeping the belts, the Wampum Keeper. And somehow or other, he talked this person into letting him have some belts.

Beauchamp then informed the state about the belts. And the state came to see if they could get the belts. And they sent a woman named Harriet Converse who told us that we should give the belts to her. This was so she could take them to Albany for safekeeping . . . because if they were here in a house, we could have a house fire, and we could lose the belts. But if we took them to Albany and put them in the museum, they would be "safe." And that wouldn't happen to them.

But shortly after the belts went up to Albany in 1911, they had a big fire in the museum there and they lost a lot of their information, their paperwork. But the belts were spared. Nothing happened to the belts. So what she was afraid of happening here at Onondaga happened in Albany. Their museum burned; they had a big fire up there. And when we're looking for information, they tell us that it was "lost in the fire."

But anyway, Harriet Converse and others came here and told us that they would keep the belts for us. And anytime we wanted to use them, we could ask for them and they'd bring them back. But once the belts left, we never saw them again. They kept the belts up in Albany, in the museum.

And in the sixties, Senator Edward Speno from Long Island was commissioned by the [New York State] Senate to repeal all laws fifty years old or older that have no relevance, no impact on today's world. So he went looking through all of them. And he was repealing these laws that were no longer useful in today's world.

And then he came across Wampum Law 27, in which the state had declared itself "Wampum Keeper" and that it could "by purchase, suit, or otherwise" obtain all belts made or to be made.* Now, I understand suing us or buying the belts, but "otherwise" opened up a whole space of how they would go about getting our belts. And I think they used the way "otherwise." Because they lied to us; they coerced us. They said, "If you don't turn the belts over, we're going to put you in jail."

And so we know that the police would come out here in the territory. And for no reason at all they would arrest our people and they'd put them in jail. And we wouldn't see them for six months or so. They'd pick them up in springtime when it was planting time. They'd pick them up during the summer when it was time to weed the gardens. They'd pick them up in the fall when it was time to harvest. So our people would be gone at these times. And they were taking care of the farms and the animals that the prisons had.

And so when they told our people that, you know, "If you don't give us the belts, we'll arrest you," our people were afraid. And I think that's how they got some of the belts. And once they took them from here, we never saw them again.

But when Edward Speno said that he was going to repeal the laws, he came across the Wampum Law 27, in which the state declared itself the Wampum Keeper. This law is unconstitutional. The state cannot make itself part of another government or religion. The law said that they could

---

* *McKinney's Consolidated Laws of New York Annotated*, "Indian Law," book 25, L. 1899, ch. 153, § 27, "Custody of Wampums" (Brooklyn, NY: Edward Thompson, 1950). The "Custody of Wampums" law was repealed in 1967.

"purchase," "sue" us, or "otherwise" get the belts from us. And he was talking to the legislators up there in Albany. And he said, "Well, what happens if I repeal this law?"

They said, "If you repeal that law, then you've got to give the belts back. So you'd better go down to Onondaga."

And so he sent a letter to us and told us what was going on. And the Onondaga leaders said, "We'll send someone up there to talk to him." So they sent me. I went up there and I spent an hour and a half with him and I explained, you know, the purpose of the belts and why it was a good idea to repeal that law and return the belts to us.

So he rewrote the law. And there were twenty-six belts up there. And he wrote the law so that all twenty-six belts came back to Onondaga. We would have got *all* of the belts back. But a man named William Fenton and another man, who worked up at the museum, had their own ideas about what they wanted to do with the belts. Fenton fought the passage of that law. By then it was in the finance committee of the [New York State] Senate. Fenton talked to his legislators and so forth. And he froze the bill in the senate. It never came out for a vote. And it had gone through the assembly and the assembly had passed the law returning all the belts to us.

But because Bill Fenton stymied the bill, and he froze it in the finance committee, the bill never came to a vote. At this time, the way the bill that was in the senate was written, all twenty-six belts would have been returned to Onondaga in 1966.

And then after that, the bill got rewritten. And every time it got rewritten, we had concerns and objections to the conditions that had been added. And we said, "No, you can't have that." So the belts were never returned.

Because of their interference in 1966, the belts were never returned until twenty-three years later. It took twenty-three years before we were able to get any of the belts. And on Oct 25, 1989, we got twelve belts back.

But I spent a lot of time with Edward Speno, you know, about the belts, and I got to meet legislators and told them about the need for us to have the belts. And why we should have them.

And then finally I talked to Marty Sullivan, who was the director of the [New York State] Museum. And I told him about the need to have those belts returned to Onondaga. And I told Marty, "The belts are our history." I explained that the belts should be returned to us so that we could explain the belts to our people, so they would understand their history.

Raymond Gonyea, an Onondaga Beaver, worked at the museum. And while he was there he explained to Marty the same thing that I told him. And between the two of us, Marty became convinced that the belts should be returned. And they looked at the laws that were written. And then Marty discovered that the museum was its own entity, and the education department was its own entity, and they didn't work under the legislation. So he didn't have to have permission from legislation to do what he wanted to do.

So what he did was, he took away the title of Wampum Keeper from the museum. And because it was no longer the Wampum Keeper, then the belts should be returned. And so he called me up and told me. And he said, "Well, we've got some papers to sign."

So I said, "All right. I'll be up."

And I took Chief Leon Shenandoah and Chief Vincent Johnson with me. And while we were up there, on a Tuesday, we signed the papers, okaying the return of the belts. And we signed an agreement that would return the title of Wampum Keeper to the Onondaga Nation. It was the ending of a long struggle to see our belts again.

And there was some paperwork with errors, and so forth. But when we got all through on Tuesday he said, "Well, when can we bring the belts back?"

The legislators started looking at their calendars. And their calendars were full all the way along. And they couldn't decide when they were going to return the belts because they wanted to come down to Onondaga, too. So we finally decided that the only day that was open was Saturday. That was four days away! And they said, "Is that all right?"

I said, "Yup, that's okay."

So I came home to Onondaga. And I said, "The belts are coming Saturday. We've got four days to invite all of the nations to come down and be here when the belts arrive." And so we did that. And we got food. We told the women they would have to be cooking that day because all the people from the Haudenosaunee nations would be coming down to see the return of the belts.

The day started out early as everyone dressed their best. We were going to burn tobacco at sunrise and later we would dance for such a great day. For the first time in almost 100 years the wampum belts were coming back to Onondaga.

We entered the longhouse at 7:00 a.m. and I put two rattles on the bench for our sacred songs. Chief Ollie Gibson went around to all of the people to gather our sacred tobacco to begin the ceremony. We followed Leon outside to burn tobacco and give thanks to the Creator for this special day.

As Faithkeeper Oren Lyons and Leon Shenandoah got ready by building a fire of apple sticks outside, the cold air and clouds reminded us of the forecast of rain and snow showers. But as Leon began the process of giving thanks that has been done by the Haudenosaunee for thousands of years, the sun began to break through the clouds. As the words and the smoke wrapped themselves around Leon on their way to the Creator, we knew it was to be a beautiful day.

The longhouse was full as Leon asked Hubert Buck and Peter Skye to sing our Great Feather Dance and he asked me to lead the dancers. We agreed. It is always a thrill to hear these sacred songs and to see the dancers. I led the dancers around the longhouse in a counter-clockwise fashion as we have always done. Everyone has their own style when they dance for the Creator and it was good to see everyone's smiling face as they danced. Sweat was streaming down our faces when the dance was done. Peter Skye then thanked the singers, dancers, and the people for coming to see the ceremony when our belts were to come home.

We got the longhouse ready for the belts. A twenty-five-foot table was set up, covered in white treaty cloth, for them. I helped sweep as more benches and chairs were brought inside. The longhouse was ready and the women were bringing their pans of food for the day's feast. The women would be ready when it came time to feed the people for the celebration.

Eleven o'clock arrived along with 600 people. The vans carrying the belts hadn't arrived and everyone was anxiously watching the road. Finally a silence fell over the crowd as someone whispered, "The belts are here!"

Looking out the longhouse window, I could see the people surrounding the vans. And they opened up the vans and the belts were all there. And they started to bring them into the longhouse. And we helped. We brought all of the belts into the longhouse.

Each belt was covered in a case. Each case was wrapped in a white foam sheet. It was impossible to tell which belt was which. The wrappings were removed and the first belt was the Thadodaho' Belt. Soon all the belts were laid out and everyone pressed forward for a better view. Our men explained that they would have opportunities to view the belts and take pictures later. We had to begin the ceremony.

The representatives from the state were seated first, along with the chiefs, clan mothers, and faithkeepers. There was not enough room for all of the people, so many stood outside. There was silence as Leon stood to give our Thanksgiving Address. His voice was the only thing heard as he mentioned all of the things that the Creator has given to us to make our life enjoyable. I stood up and introduced the member nations of the Haudenosaunee. All of the nations had sent representatives to the ceremony.

Then I introduced Martin Sullivan, director of the New York State Museum in Albany. Martin greeted the Haudenosaunee. He explained about the meetings that led up to this day and how it was time for the belts to be returned to the Haudenosaunee. He then introduced the commissioner of education, Thomas Sobol. Thomas explained his part in the exchange of custody of the belts and how he saw this as a new beginning in the relationship of our people. Martin Sullivan then introduced the chancellor of regents. The chancellor explained the condolence cane and how the drawings represent the leaders of the Haudenosaunee.

Then the secretary of state, Gail Schaffer, was introduced. Gail explained that Governor Mario Cuomo could not attend, but that he was sending his regards on such an important day. She said that the state had much to learn from Native Americans—they have made many contributions to the state and the world, including the foundations of democratic forms of government.

Martin Sullivan then stated that he had been given the Wampum Keeper's Collar a few days before; it has been with the state since 1900. Since the State was no longer the Wampum Keeper, Martin was returning the collar to the Onondagas. He then placed the collar around Leon's neck. This ended the speeches from the state.

Leon stood and, in the language of the Onondagas, he thanked the people for the belts. Audrey Shenandoah interpreted what he said into English. She explained that the Creator had sent messages to us and that we must carry these messages to the people. We were given a way to record these messages. That was placing the messages into wampum strings or belts. She explained how Leon spoke of our way of life and how important it was to continue on the path our Creator has shown us.

I then explained that after the Revolutionary War, some of our people moved north to what is now Canada. In 1988, the trustees of the [then] Museum of the American Indian returned eleven belts to the people at Grand River. I explained that some of the people from Grand River were here to help us celebrate the return of the belts to Onondaga. Then I introduced Chief Jake Thomas.

Jake spoke to the people assembled. After he finished, he said he would translate what he said. He explained that these belts present a visual document of our history and the formation of the Haudenosaunee. It would take a long time to explain each of the belts. "Today is not the time to do this," he said.

Jake Thomas then said that he hoped that we would all learn from these belts but that he must stop talking, for he noticed that Leon was checking his watch, which meant that he was hungry and wanted to eat! He ended by stating that the twelve belts were returned to Onondaga and that maybe they would think about returning our land.

I then informed the people that it was time to go outside where Chief Jake Swamp of the Mohawk Nation would plant the Tree of Peace—the tree that Commissioner Thomas Sobol had presented to Leon when we signed the agreement. Jake has performed this tree-planting ceremony all over the world, spreading the good words of our Peacemaker. The tree was exceptionally beautiful as everyone put a shovelful of dirt around it. It was cold and the wind was brisk, but the people stood as history was repeated: the Tree of Peace was again being planted at Onondaga.

We returned back to the longhouse to dance. I knew that this event would be remembered for a lifetime, especially by our white brothers who had never had the opportunity to see the Round Dance before today. I joined Hubert Buck, Jerry McDonald, Robert Shenandoah, and others on the bench to sing. Everyone held hands as they formed a circle and danced around us. After the dance ended, Leon thanked the Creator for all of the living things that make life a joy. I reminded the people that we should work for the day when there would be peace throughout the world and that the Four Protectors would look after everyone as they journeyed home.

People then went into the cookhouse for a meal that would also be held in memory. Buffalo, deer, and turkey meats were accompanied by potatoes, squash, pumpkin, cranberries, and salads for the hungry people. The food covered the tables. Hot scones were plentiful and cold strawberry drink was there to quench everyone's thirst.

The belts remained on display until 5:00 p.m. Many took pictures, viewed, and asked questions about the belts. Most stood in awe at the sight of our twelve belts coming home. The press were there and they took pictures, as well. At 8:00 p.m., we danced various social dances until 11:30 p.m. Some of our Albany visitors soon joined us even though they didn't know how to do the steps. We all had a good time.

Leon then gave the Thanksgiving, which ended our day. It was easy to see that this was a day that would not be forgotten and would be told to our children and our grandchildren. It was a great day! We gave our thanks.

So the belts got returned and they've been with us since. They were gone from about 1890 to 1989, almost 100 years. So it was a big day for us to have those belts returned.

And of the twenty-six belts, what came back to us were twelve belts, meaning there were fourteen belts that were left up there in the museum. And those fourteen belts are still there at Albany. Because back then, the state not only went to us, but they went to all the other nations and picked up belts. That's why there were twenty-six belts up there.

And the Mohawks are still trying to get the ones that belonged to them out of there and they've been unable to get them. The state won't give them back to the Mohawks, just like they wouldn't give them to us over all of these years. So I don't know how that's going to be.

It's been a long fight. And it took me from 1966 until '89 to get the belts back. That's over twenty years. When they came back, oh what a grand feeling that was! It was a historic day. And when that day happened, I said, "If the people who had been fighting to get the belts returned all of these years were here, they would feel this was a great day."

The butternut trees

In the issue of land claims of the Haudenosaunee, some of the discussion has been about the size of the territory of the Haudenosaunee. And there are various ways of figuring out how big the territory was. Historians have written that the territory of the Haudenosaunee was larger than the Roman Empire. It stretched from Canada down to the Carolinas, and from the Atlantic Ocean over to the Mississippi—an area bigger than the Roman Empire.

All controlled without an army, just by the Great Law, the peace law, the Great Peace. If you're coming in and living with us, then this is the way you will live: there'll be no wars; there'll be no fighting. So there were no wars and no fighting within our territories during this time, for over 2,000 years.

And so the historians then debate, well, how did they determine their territories? How big were their territories? And at a land rights session at Colgate University, William Starna from Oneonta said, "It's easy to figure out how much territory the Haudenosaunee controlled or lived in," he said, "because the individual Indian ate three and a half deer a year."

Now how he figured this out, I have no idea. But that's what he said: "They had three and a half deer a year."

I said, "So a village of 1,000 people would need three and a half deer each or would require 3,500 deer." Now 3,500 deer out of a herd every year would have to be such that it didn't hurt the herd. The herd could continue. Even if you took 3,500 deer out of the herd, the herd would continue.

And so Bill Starna said, "One deer needs 'x' amount of acres of land in order for him to feed." So you take the amount of acreage that a deer needs and multiply it by the amount of deer that you need. And that determines the size of the territory of that village or that nation. So if you've got 1,000 people, you've got 3,500 deer. And 3,500 deer need "x" amount of acreage in order to survive. But they need a bigger herd than 3,500, so you take that number and multiply it by the acreage. And that would give you the territory.

I said, "Well, there's another way to determine Haudenosaunee territory. And that's with the butternut trees. The Haudenosaunee have always had butternuts. And wherever they went, they took the butternuts with them and they planted them. So anytime you find butternut trees, you know this was the territory of the Haudenosaunee.

"And they grow along the St. Lawrence River over to the Hudson River, down the Hudson River, over to the Mississippi and up around Chicago, and so forth. All butternut trees. This is the area, the property of the Haudenosaunee, wherever these butternuts grow."

And I said, "It's a huge area—from the Mississippi to the Hudson River, from Canada down to the Carolinas." I said, "And we still harvest the butternuts. Right now on my porch hangs a bag full of butternuts for my eating pleasure this winter."

So I tell the people that dig up graves, "Don't dig me up to find out whether I eat corn and butternuts, because I'll tell you now that I eat butternuts. But if anybody's looking to see if I do this, I'll tell you now, so you won't do that after I die!"

Speaking American

I had a presentation at one time that I made in Cortland, Hobart, Cornell, Colgate, and Syracuse University. And my idea was to show the students that the United States does not qualify to be in the United Nations.

And this is the way it started: "There are stipulations or criteria as to how you can become a member of the United Nations. You have to have a government and leaders. You need to have a land base. You need a judicial system and a language. But the United States does not have an official language."

And under this, the Onondaga Nation and the Haudenosaunee could be a member of the United Nations. (But we won't, because of the status and stipulations. And our leader says, "No, we can't go into that kind of situation." We are going to maintain our status.)

But anyway, I made this speech at these universities. And two weeks after I made the speech at SU, I read in the paper that the United States had passed a law making English the official language of the United States!

Now I maintain that this is not true, because the citizens of the United States are not speaking English. They speak American, which has no foundation. English is founded on French and Latin. And it has rules as to how words are formed, made, and interpreted. American does not have that, does not have a root; it doesn't have any rules and regulations. They violate the English language all the time. And it's very hard to determine how to pronounce words because of the usage of the alphabet.

For instance, the letters *mi* are pronounced two different ways. Depending upon where they are, they're pronounced like the word "me" or the word "my." "Me" and "my" for *mi*. (And it's not just *mi*, there are other places where the *i* is used with another letter and it's pronounced two different ways.)

So I was driving through Florida. And I was coming into this town. And I didn't know whether I was coming into "my-ah-my" or "me-ah-me." And I stopped at a gas station for gas. And I asked him where I was. And he told me I was in "my-am-me," which they spell *Miami*.

So I said, "They use *mi* in both ways in this word." Because we're speaking American, they use both pronunciations: it's "my-am-me."

And then what they do there is they sound the second *m* twice. They use the second *m* with the *a* that's in the middle for the syllable of "am," like "I am." And then they use another *m* with the last letter *i* for the syllable "me." So it's not "my-ah-my" or "me-ah-me," it's "my-a*m-m*e" (Miami). But that's American for you, rather than English!

Learn everything you can about *both*: our ways and the European's ways

The Revolutionary War is only one of the traumatic things that have happened to us since the newcomers arrived. Another one is boarding schools. The European people came in and said, "Now we've got to educate these people." We didn't realize, of course, that the education of our people in boarding schools was a plan to remove us from who we were to be something like they were: English-speaking people who were educated in schools. But no longer talking a Native language, no longer doing ceremonies, in fact no longer Native.

Being Native or Haudenosaunee was a problem to them. And so as you look back historically you see these commissions that are put up to take care of the "Indian problem." And we were the "problem." And so all of these things that happened back then impacted us. They impacted our people. And because of those things that impacted us, changes were made in the people themselves. And today some of our people, who are doing studies on this, figure that those traumatic events that happened in our lives still affect us.

This boarding school concept was a way . . . I guess we refer to it today as genocide: destroying the culture through education. They wanted to assimilate us into their way. So if they could do that, it would mean they would change us to be something like they were. And they would then be able to control us.

In 1890, General Henry B. Errol Carrington came in among the Haudenosaunee. As a "special agent" gathering information for the United States Census, he took notes about our people—a census, a check on who is around. He counted the amount of people. He counted who went to school and who didn't go to school. Here at Onondaga the average number of days that our children spent in school was about twenty days a year. They just would not go to school. And only a few of them spoke English.

In 1800, a Seneca man, a prophet, was giving our people a message that he received. And he said that, in that message, he saw a school. In the school were children who were crying and they couldn't get out. And so he said that we should learn enough about education and the white man so that we would be able to deal with him. Now in 1800, knowing a little bit of English so that you could get by was okay. We were already through with our treaties because we had started our treaties in 1784, 1789, and 1794. And through interpreters and so forth we were able to get by. Those treaties are still in effect, ratifying the means by which we can ensure the preservation of us as a people.

When I became a chief—one of the leaders here at Onondaga—in 1964, the people that I was sitting there and talking with were talking about treaties and treaty obligations and what the United States was supposed to be doing. And what they were not doing. And so I went out and I looked for the treaties. What treaties were they talking about? I found them [in Syracuse] in the library down at the corner of Salina and Colvin. I couldn't take the books out, but I could sit there and I could read them. And so I looked at these treaties. I copied them down and I brought them back to the Council. And I said, "The treaty obligations that you're talking about are not in the written version of the treaties."

And they said, "They're not?"

And I said, "No. Has anyone ever read a treaty?"

And they said, "No."

And I said, "Well, then let's read one."

So we went through the federal treaties. This was 1964. So from 1964 to today, 2004, we've had mucho problems with the state and the federal government. There are court decisions coming at us. We have to hire lawyers. And the more that we get involved with this, the more educated we have to be.

And my dad was like one of those people described in the 1890 census. There were only a few that were going to school. And the average was twenty days a year. When you say 1890, you know, that's a long time ago, ancient history—until you figure it out mathematically. My father was born in 1905, which is fifteen years after the 1890 census. He's not in the census, but his sister, Jesse, is. She's in the census and Jesse died a few years ago. My father passed away a few years ago. But his mother and father and his brothers are in the 1890 census. So it's not that long ago when they're talking about who we were and what we were about and the education of our people.

But as we moved out into today's world, my dad was one of the leaders. And when the legal stuff came in, because he only had a fourth grade education, he didn't understand it. There would be English words there and he wouldn't know what they meant.

So we would sit and we would talk. And I would explain. And I'm not what you would call formally educated. I'm not a college graduate; I'm a high school graduate. But I'm very fortunate in that the Creator gave me a gift of being able to communicate and to remember. And so when I would read things, I would remember.

And my dad and I used to sit down, and he would explain oral history to me. And I would explain written history to him. And I would decipher it the best I could, what the English words meant and what was being said on the pieces of paper.

So as we did this we found out that the more we know about how they [the non-Native people] operate and what they say, the better we are able to protect ourselves. And because of this, when I got married and had children, I was telling them, "You have to educate yourself, you know."

I said, "You have to be able to learn about them, what they're about, how they operate, so that you can go out there and work. But you also have to bring knowledge back and work in the community so that we can protect ourselves. Because the number one priority in this whole scheme of things is to preserve the Onondagas as a people and to preserve the Haudenosaunee and to make sure that the gifts and the messages that we received 2,000 years ago, 1,000 years ago, 200 years ago from the Messengers—the Peacemaker and Handsome Lake—continue.

"Because without the continuation of those ceremonies, those songs, those dances and those teachings, we no longer would be who we are:

Onondagas, Onoñda'gegá', or Onkwehonwe, or Haudenosaunee. So that's the top priority."

So there's a big debate among the people as to whether education is *bad* for you. Well, anything is bad for you if it's in excess. One of the things that came in with the Europeans is the fiddle. And so Handsome Lake in the 1800s said, "The fiddle is not for you. You shouldn't be doing those things."

Well, the reason why he said that is because people were going to dances, they were square dancing. So the fiddle was one of those instruments. But it also could be a trumpet. It could be anything that takes you away from the longhouse and takes you away from the path of the Creator. Liquor, drugs, TV, radio, things that change your mind—the mind changers, they call them—will move you away from that. So those aren't good.

And education . . . if you educate yourself and all the education you get is European education, white education, then that's what you are. You're not Native anymore because you don't know all of your history, you don't know these things. You have to educate yourself in both ways. So the debate among the Natives, especially the older Natives, is that they did not believe in education. Leon Shenandoah, our last Thadodaho', was deadly against education. "We don't need education. I went through life . . . I don't need education and I did fine, you know, I worked and I got. . . ."

Well, you worked, yeah, but in today's world you need to have an education because today if you have to go out off the territory to work, you can't get a job unless you've got a high school education. And if you have a high school education, you are limited in where you can go on the outside. If you go to college, you make much more money. And then that's a bachelor's degree. And if you get a master's degree, that's more. If you get a doctor's degree, a PhD, you make even more, depending on what field and the circumstances. A few years ago we had, in California, people with PhDs walking up and down the street with no job. And that's the economics of the world.

And so because of this, I taught my children about who they are. So Nancy, Bradley, Barry, and Neal have been taught the Longhouse ways.

They participate in the ceremonies. They sing the songs that are there in the longhouse. They do all of these things, but they're also educated. Nancy has a master's degree in education. Barry has three and a half years at Syracuse University. Bradley has a master's degree in education and he's certified both in education and special education. Neal has a bachelor's degree in psychology. Bradley's wife has a bachelor's degree in education. Neal's wife has a degree in law. And this is necessary if you're in the outside world.

So there are two educations that are here, and the *most* important is the education of the Haudenosaunee and the Onondagas if we are to preserve our heritage and culture. And second is the education of the white man, because we have to learn how they think, how they act, so that we can protect ourselves against the things that are coming.

For instance, in 1788 the Onondagas made a treaty with New York State. Line one says the Onondagas hereby cede to the state of New York all of their lands. So a couple of years ago, we were sitting in the longhouse looking at this treaty. And one of our leaders said, "Yes, we seed our land every spring. We plant corn, beans, squash, cucumbers, and everything. We always seed our garden."

But the word in the treaty is "cede," meaning you're *giving up*. And the other word is "seed," which means you're *planting seeds*. And if you don't know that—the difference between the two words—then you get problems when you sit down and talk with the scholars and the state and the federal government. Because they have a language—the English language—that's tough to understand sometimes. So it's necessary for us to learn both ways, to be educated in both, in order to survive as a people.

And what's not in the textbooks is the oral history. Oral history can tell us about what used to be, compared to what's here today. And acid rain is one of the big issues in the watershed. And Oren said, "Well, a long time ago"—a long time ago being [the time of] my dad and his dad—"they used to leave here from across the road and walk up over this hill and down the other side. And there they would spear fish." My dad said the fish were so plentiful going up that river that it looked like you could walk across their backs. Now I never saw this, but when he told about it, he said,

"We used to go up there; we'd take a burlap bag and we'd come back with a whole bag full of fish."

And then they'd just walk around the community and give fish away to everybody. This is the concept—the idea—that when you're out hunting and you have all this, that you share this with the people when you come back, you know. A lot of old people aren't able to hunt or fish, so you do that. And so when I grew up, my dad told me about these things. And this is the way we are.

So my dad would tell me the oral history of our people, as a people. And oral history's not in the books.

Oren Lyons went to school up until the eighth grade. He quit school and he bummed around during World War II and up to 1950. In 1950 he enlisted and served in the Korean War for four years. He came out. We were playing lacrosse against Syracuse University and Oren was in the goal. So Roy Simmons Sr. was the coach up there at SU and he said, "Oren," he said, "we'd like to have you in the nets here at SU. How about coming into school up here?"

And Oren said, "Sure. That'd be good."

And so Roy Simmons Sr. said, "Well, get your papers together and then come up and take the test."

So Oren showed up at SU, an eighth-grader with no record of being in high school at all. Eighth grade is only junior high. He never went to ninth grade—ninth, tenth, eleventh, or twelfth. He never went to school. And so he said, "I don't know where my papers are. I can't find them."

Well, he didn't have any! He took the test. He passed the test. He gets into college and he's there for four years. He graduates from SU.

And he's sitting in a boat on Otisco Lake with my dad. And my dad says, "Well," he says, "you've graduated from college."

And Oren says, "Yes, I did."

And he says, "Well, good." Then he says, "Who are you now?"

And Oren says, "Well, who am I?" (A trick question, you know.)

Oren's sitting there. And my dad's just staring at him. And Oren says, "Well, I'm Oren Lyons. I'm Wolf Clan. And I'm Seneca."

"And?"

"Well, I'm a graduate of Syracuse University. And I got a job. I'm going down to New York."

"And?"

And, you know, so Oren is thinking. And he goes through a whole bunch of stuff, you know, figuring that he's answering my father's question. But every time he finished talking, my father would say, "And?"

And Oren finally ran out of things to say. And he says, "Well, that's it. That's who I am."

And my dad says, "No." He says, "Look across the lake," he says, "and tell me what you see."

"Well," Oren says, "there's a big hill there. There are trees; there are stones; there are flowers. And the hill is huge, you know. And it comes down, right down to the water level, you know." He says, "That's what I see."

And my dad says, "Well, that's who you are. You *are* those trees. You are those stones. You are the water. And you are the hill. You are the wind. You are the elements of the environment. That's who you are. You're Seneca, you're Haudenosaunee, but you're the people of the land. That's who you are."

And when you look at yourself this way, you realize that what my father was saying is that everything is connected. My father never read Chief Seattle's speech. I don't even know if he knew about it. But in the 1850s, Chief Seattle reminded the Europeans who were coming into the territory that whatever you do to the web, like a spider web, you know, you do to yourself.

And he was explaining that, you know, you can't go around and pollute the water. You can't go around and pollute the air. You can't kill all the animals. You can't do all of these things because this is part of nature. This is part of who we are. And whatever you do to these elements—the buffalo, the deer, the trees, the water, and so forth—if you destroy and pollute, you destroy or pollute some of yourself.

After a meeting with the EPA and the DEC, one of the elders in Onondaga was talking to his nephew. And his nephew, who was at the meeting, said, you know, "You're an environmentalist." And the elder said, "No, I'm not an environmentalist. I can't be, because I *am* the environment."

So when Oren was speaking to the UN, they asked him, they said, "Who are you speaking for?"

He said, "I'm here to speak on behalf of the buffalo and the eagle who have lost their voice." And he said, "They are becoming endangered because of what is going on in the world," he said, "and I'm here to tell you that we have to change our ways. Otherwise we're going to lose the animal world."

But this all comes from my dad's teachings and his father's teachings.

And my dad said to me, "When you're out hunting," he said, "shoot only what you need, when you need it. And whatever you shoot, make sure that you use it. And use everything that you can of that, whatever it is."

So when I went hunting, I shot a rabbit. I brought *a* rabbit home. We ate the rabbit. I would go back out and shoot another rabbit. I would shoot a pheasant. I would shoot a deer, and I wouldn't go hunting again until I needed something.

Now when Nancy and Barry were growing up, we had pheasant every Sunday. There were pheasants here at Onondaga. There are no pheasants here today because the environment has changed. There are no longer the farms; the cornfields aren't here, and so there are no pheasants here. So the young people today have never tasted a pheasant. They don't know what it's like.

And there are no fish in the streams in the numbers that my father talked about, when you could walk across their backs, they were so plentiful.

But we had—me and my wife, Helen, and Barry, Brad, Nancy, and Neal—we had pheasant every Sunday. I had raccoons in the freezer. I had deer in the freezer, and we had rabbit stew. But all the time I remembered my father's words, "Take only what you need, when you need it, and make sure that you use whatever you take." And this is an unwritten law.

But the Europeans who come into our territory can't live that way. If they're given the choice, they would take all of the fish. They would take all of the rabbits. They would take all of the pheasants. They would take all of the deer. There wouldn't be any. They would shoot them all. They almost exterminated the buffalo. They did exterminate many species, such as the homing pigeon. And it's sad when you think about that, you know, that you had all of these pigeons and they were so plentiful. And then the guns came in and the Europeans just shot them, and now we don't have any.

So, I'll leave you with that: as you progress through life, learn everything you can about *both*, our ways and the European's ways, so that we can preserve ourselves as a people.

"Randomly" audited

In 1966, when I was arguing with the state of New York over taxation, I was using the freedom of speech [the protection of freedom of speech in the First Amendment of the Constitution]. And because I was using the freedom of speech, the state of New York had no way to stop me. And they had the same problem with Al Capone, the gangster from Chicago. He was doing a lot of illegal stuff, but for some reason or other, they couldn't get him. So they sent the IRS [Internal Revenue Service] after him and they got him on tax evasion. And they put him in jail for that reason.

Now, in '66, when I was speaking, all I was doing was putting the truth out, about laws. I wasn't *violating* any laws. And the state didn't know how to stop me. So they sent the IRS.

And this is odd . . . I think that everybody knows that now and then you can get audited by the IRS about your income tax. And they will randomly pick your name out of the so-called box where all the names of the people that are filing income tax are. And they will take that name and they will decide that they will audit that person.

Because I was such a problem for the state, because of what I was doing with their state laws and so forth, they sent the IRS. And I was audited *eight* years in a row. How you get "randomly" picked eight years in a row is beyond. . . .

Now at this time, there were no civil liberties. There were none of these nonprofit advocates that would help people out when they are in a bind legally and so forth. So I was all by myself. And it was really no big problem because I had filed. They said I didn't. I said I did. And they audited me, which only meant that when I filed, they sent me a notice that they were auditing me. So instead of getting my tax refund in April or May, I got it in November.

And they not only came after me, but they came after the people who I was associating with. Dr. Robert W. Venables—a history professor who was working with me, trying to get history out correctly—he got audited twice. Oren Lyons, my cousin, also got audited.

So when I decided that I should point out to the people that the United States did not qualify to be in the United Nations, I was looking towards maybe getting the United States out of the UN. And I presented at Hobart, Cortland, Cornell, Colgate, and Syracuse University. And after I presented at SU, the United States—*probably*, I say—was informed of what I was doing and what I was saying. And so, as I was saying earlier, two weeks later they got Congress to pass a law making English the official language of the United States. So they would now qualify to be in the United Nations.

Which is very interesting, to me, to think that from 1966 to 1970-something, these people were still following me around, checking up on what I was doing and what I was saying. Because I was making a presentation that the United States did not qualify to be in the UN. So they passed a law making themselves qualified. A very interesting turn of events!

Condemned to repeat history

Earlier, I talked about Washington's empire. Along the same issue as to whether the United States exists or New York State exists is another political entity called an empire. In 1783, George Washington, standing on the banks of Oneida Lake, said, as he looked west, "I think I will build an empire out of all of this land that extends west." And he had started building his empire, previous to that, in 1779.

The only way that he could build an empire was by getting rid of all the Native people on the land. And so in 1783 he set up a genocide policy to get rid of all of the Native people so that he could build his empire. And he started doing that in 1779 when he sent John Sullivan into Cayuga and Seneca country, and when he sent Goose van Schaick into our Onondaga country. And Van Schaik and his men came around the northern side of Oneida Lake and attacked the Onondaga towns and killed all the people they could.

And the people ran away. And then he said, "Well, there are people out there that I didn't get. So what I'll do is I'll remove their food supply so they'll starve to death." So he burned our orchards; he burned all of our food that we had stored for the winter. And because he did this, we named George Washington "Hanadaga·yas," which means "town destroyer."

And because it is our policy to pass names on from generation to generation, we refer to every president of the United States as "Hanadaga·yas." And if you look at the history of American presidents, you will find that they have destroyed many towns. Andrew Jackson, Nixon, Truman— Truman dropped two bombs on Japan, killing *thousands* of people and destroying two towns, Nagasaki and Hiroshima, and injuring thousands of people. So the name Hanadaga·yas fits the president of the United

States. And Washington, DC, has an Indian name also. And it means "where Hanadaga·yas lives."

I was sitting here one day thinking about Europe. I said, "You know, I've got German people coming here. I'm on the cover of a book in Czechoslovakia. Italians come here. French people come here. And these are now countries that were in what was known, a long time ago, as the Roman Empire. Who does not come to my house are Romans." And I wondered why. So doing the research, I find out that the Roman Empire collapsed.

Further research shows that Alexander the Great, in the year 300, was expanding his empire. And he went into the Middle East. And when he got there his empire collapsed.

Other empires also went into the Middle East and their empires collapsed. So much so that the Middle East became known as the "graveyard of empires." And where's the United States today? They are in the Middle East. And so I reported this to some students at SU. A year after I told that to the students, Wall Street collapsed. So I went back there and I said, "Well, Wall Street is the beginning of the collapse of your empire."

I was sitting there listening to the radio one day and it said the Russian empire has collapsed. And then I heard the Japanese empire collapsed and I said, to myself, *So empires are still collapsing.*

And then, one day, on the newsstands was the *New York Times*, their newspaper.* And on the front it said, "Why Empires Collapse." And they listed a bunch of empires that collapsed. And the bottom line said, "Will the USA be next?" And this was after I had made my statement. So someone is doing research also and coming to the same conclusion that I've come to, that the United States is going to collapse.

Now how bad it's going to be, I have no idea. It's like a snowstorm. Wall Street was your indication that it's coming. What comes next, we don't know how bad it's going to be or how long it's going to last. But it will be worse than Wall Street.

---

* John Noble Wilford, "Collapse of Earliest Known Empire Is Linked to Long, Harsh Drought," *New York Times*, August 24, 1993, C1 and C10.

And I can say these things because a Spanish-American philosopher [George Santayana], born in Spain in 1863, wrote in 1905 that people who do not study and learn from history are condemned to repeat it. And if the United States doesn't study why Rome, Russia, and Japan, and all these other empires collapsed, and take steps so that they don't do those things, it is destined to collapse. And I don't suppose they even realize that they are an empire or they're progressing to be an empire because the statement that is made by George Washington in 1783 is probably not known by them—the statement that he was starting out to build his empire.

Which explains why, when New York State started making treaties and taking land and adding it on to what they call the state of New York, all of those treaties were illegal. They were a violation of the articles of the Constitution and the 1768 treaty with England. The Constitution says that the only people who can make a treaty with a foreign nation is the United States. And the Haudenosaunee are a foreign nation. And so all of those treaties that New York State made as the state of New York were illegal because of the articles of the Constitution that say they're not authorized to do that.

And George Washington knew that this was happening. He knew the treaties were illegal and all the negotiations were illegal. But he allowed it to go through because he was building his empire. So he understood what was going on, but whether he passed that information on down to others, I have no idea. Because from what we see in Washington, DC, when the president leaves, he folds up his book and he takes all his papers with him. So the information that preceded the incoming president is not known.

George Washington's statement that he was building an empire probably just stayed with him. But the statement *was* made and the United States *was* building an empire. They went into the Caribbean. They went to the Hawaiian Islands and they extended their empire. They made the Hawaiian Islands a state, which added to their empire.

Then they went to Alaska and they added that to their empire. And now they're in the Middle East. And they're doing the same thing in the Middle East as the Russians did when they were in the Middle East. The Russians were spreading communism as a form of government that the people should follow. The United States is saying, "We have a government; you should follow our way, because it's a good way." So they're doing the same thing that Russia did. And I heard on the radio the Russian empire collapsed. So how soon will it be before the United States empire collapses? And how will it collapse? Politically, spiritually, environmentally, agriculturally, financially? There are all different ways it could collapse.

According to that Spanish-American philosopher, the United States empire is going to collapse because they haven't studied why empires collapse. And they're doing the same thing all those other empires did, so they're condemned to repeat history.

Referees

I'd like to mention a group of people that make me wonder who they are. And these are referees at a football game. These people—you can see them, they'll take off their baseball caps . . . they're baldheaded or they've got white hair and they're refereeing a game that could be high school, college, or professional—any one of those. But all the players are young players. And the college teams have track stars on their teams that are able to run the 100-yard dash in just a few seconds.

And so they get in their huddle, they line up, they give the ball to the quarterback, he fades back, and running down the sidelines is one of these track stars. And the quarterback throws a pass and the track star catches the ball at the goal line. And he gets tackled. But guess who's standing on the sidelines watching this whole play? It's the referee, one of these old guys.

He's down there *before* the track star is there. And he's there to determine whether he caught the ball in-bounds, out-of-bounds, if it is actually a touchdown, or he got tackled. But he's there before anyone else. He's there when the play happens. And he does this not only on forward passes, but he also does it on running plays. The quarterback will give it to the tight end. The tight end makes a wide sweep around, runs down the sidelines. And—you've watched TV—the referee is running alongside of him making sure that when the play ends he can definitely say where the ball goes or who has possession of it, in case there's a fumble.

And so I'm watching this. And I know that these guys are not the same age as the players. So it makes me wonder, *Who are these people anyway that can keep up with all these young guys?*

You see my wonderments are not all bad!

He said, "I can document your oral tradition"

Now back to the discussion about our first treaty with the Netherlands in the early 1600s. And in order to explain more about it, I'll tell you what happened in 1972. In 1972, there was a knock on my door. And I went to the door, opened the door and this man was standing there. And he said, "I'm Dr. Robert Venables from Oswego State Teachers College. I'm a history professor. And I'd like to sit down and talk to you."

I said, "Well, come on in. Have a cup of coffee."

And I told him, "Bob, this is what happened."

In 1972 he said, "I never heard of that."

"Well," I said, "this is part of our history."

So he went away. But then he would come back, and we would talk again. After a few visits, he began saying, "Irv, here is your documentation of what you were telling me about. I can document your oral tradition."

Now ever since then to today we still do this. Every Friday he comes to my house. And we sit and we talk about history. Thirty-five years we've been doing this. It's fun to sit with Bob Venables. We talk about oral history—my oral history—and he tells me about his history. And in most cases, he can verify my oral history.

There'll come a time when we will have our belt, but you won't have your piece of paper

So a couple of months ago we were sitting there. And we were talking about the very first international treaty I referred to earlier, made in the early 1600s with the Dutch. And what happened was that because of our process, and the language that was going on, our people there at this meeting said, "We should record this."

And the Dutch people said, "Well, we have a pen and paper. And we'll write this down."

And we said, "That's okay for you, but we have a way of recording also. We make wampum belts. And this is our history. So that's what we'll do. And we think that in the future, there'll come a time when we will have our belt, but you won't have your piece of paper."

And I've been saying this for years. And I lecture at different colleges. And I bring this Two Row Wampum Belt with me. It's an agreement where we would live together and we record this under the natural laws. And we will preserve what's here today for future generations.

And so anyway, I sat down with Bob. And we talked about this treaty and what was said. . . .

And also back there in '72, I got a phone call from a guy in Pennsylvania who said, "I've got some important papers for you. Will you come down and get them?"

I said, "All right." So I sent my father and Lee Lyons down to Pennsylvania. They picked up this paper and brought it back. And the paper that they brought back was a paper written in old Dutch. And it told about this agreement that was made between the Dutch people and the Haudenosaunee.

And in 1980 we sent a delegation over to the Netherlands. And I said, "Well, as long as you're going over there, take this paper with you. And see if they can interpret what's on it." So they took the paper with them and they talked to the mayor of The Hague.

And he said, "Oh, this is in old Dutch. I can't read it," he said, "but I will get it interpreted for you." And so they did that.

Now at the beginning it gives some names of the people who were coming over from the Netherlands to see about a trade agreement. It says that they have a piece of paper that authorizes them to negotiate a trade agreement with the residents of the "New World." And the names that are on that paper were then researched by them over there in the Netherlands. One of the names was the captain who brought his ship from the Netherlands to the "New World." So the names on there are actual people from the Netherlands.

I said, "Wow! Isn't that something!" So we have a document now that verifies this agreement that was made that I have in the wampum belt.

So a few months ago, I said, "Bob, I have these papers that were given to me back in 1972 by a man named Van Loon." So Bob went into his computer and researched the Cornell library. And he came back to me two weeks later. He found references to it in later treaties and in publications of *The Indian Historian* in San Francisco. "Irv," he said, "here are documents that verify the treaty you were talking about." So he handed me this piece of paper with these names on it that I had presented to the Netherlands back in 1980. He had the same paper, only it was done up in English and dated April 21st, 1613.

So he said, "Here, this verifies your oral history." Some white scholars reject the 1613 treaty. But we have the Two Row.

This document is available on the Internet. So if you want to read about this, you can. And with Bob's help, we can, in most cases, verify the oral history that I talked about.

Anyway, back in the early 1600s, we talked about how we would coexist—we would protect the earth, waters, animals, and so forth. And we agreed that we would live side-by-side; we would coexist and we would not pass laws to govern the other one.

What if we should pass a law that you can't do that anymore? Would that be acceptable?

Now the Haudenosaunee have never violated this treaty. We have never passed a law telling you people how to live or what to do, or how or what you can't do. Your nation, on the other hand, has lost the meaning of this treaty and you violate this treaty every day. You pass laws that say we can't do this, we can't do that, we can't go here, we can't go there.

You have laws that say the Lakotas can't go into the Black Hills. That's their sacred ground. They've been going there for thousands of years to do their ceremonies and so forth. And you've got a federal law that says they can't go there. And that's a violation of that Two Row Wampum Belt.

You have laws that say we can't perform ceremonies. And the reason why you do this is because you don't understand why we do these things. You say to yourselves, "They sing songs, they dance, and do these things. We don't understand that, so let's pass a law that says they can't do that anymore."

Now how does that work on the other side if we pass laws that say *you* can't do things?

How many get Easter baskets on Easter? How many are going to—when they get married, or have children—are going to give Easter baskets on Easter? Why do you do that? And why do you put a chocolate bunny rabbit in there with jellybeans? Why does a chocolate bunny rabbit bring jellybeans on Easter? Do you people know?

Well, we don't know either! It sort of makes me wonder who are these people anyway! So, what if we should pass a law that you can't do that anymore? Would that be acceptable?

No. So now you know what I mean when I say you're passing laws that tell me I can't do things.

But that's a prime example of how this Two Row Wampum Belt should work. We must respect each other as people with different languages, different cultures, different governments.

You have a government. You have leaders. You have a way of life. And so do we. We have leaders. We have ways to put them in. We have a judicial system, and it's been there for a long time. And just because you have laws and you have a big country and 300 million people in it, it does not give you the right to change my way of life.

When you do this, you violate that early treaty.

Now what happened was, as we made these treaties, we recorded them with our wampum belts. In the longhouse at Onondaga there is a picture of the November 11th, 1794 Treaty at Canandaigua. And that treaty, made in 1794, is a belt that is six foot long. It's about six inches wide. It has a number of figures on it. It has a figure of a house in the middle and two figures alongside of it.

And there are different interpretations of what those mean. But one interpretation says that one of the figures is Thadadaho? [the leader of the Haudenosaunee] and that the other one is George Washington, sitting alongside the longhouse of the Haudenosaunee as they sat down and made this agreement. Even though this agreement was signed on November 11th, 1794, the people who sat down to make it sat down in July. So July, August, September, October, and November they sat and they discussed this peace treaty.

That peace treaty in 1794 has gone through the process in Washington, DC, where it's been ratified by Congress. That treaty is still in effect. And that treaty was a peace treaty, so that the people who were coming into our territory would have free passage through our territory. They promised us at that time that they would build roads through our territory. The roads would then be free to us to travel on at no cost. They would build them and they would maintain them. And we would never have to pay a toll on those roads.

If you get a copy of the November 11th, 1794 Treaty of Canandaigua—the treaties are accessible on the Internet—there is a sentence in there that says going from point "a" to Buffalo there is a toll road. And the Natives will not have to pay a toll on that road. And that was the intent of the treaty, so that the United States could build roads through our territory and we would have free passage, safe passage through our territory. Now when they built the toll thruway, those people forgot about these treaties. They charge us for traveling on that road.

So, as I said earlier, it's important for us as Native people to understand the treaties and the *intent* of the treaties. And to teach the US citizens about these treaties so that they understand that they have obligations to their treaties that are still in effect.

The Haudenosaunee have treaties with Great Britain, the Dutch, and the United States. And the United States treaties are still in effect. They have gone through the process that a treaty must go through. It goes through the House of Representatives, the Senate, and so forth. There's a process that verifies a treaty. And all of the treaties that we have, have gone through this process.

So the Fort Stanwix Treaty of 1784, the Fort Harmar Treaty of 1789, and the Canandaigua Treaty of 1794 are still in effect. In fact, the 1794 treaty stipulates that $4,500 will be expended annually and be given to the Haudenosaunee for the purchase of goods, machinery, seeds, chickens, and animals for farming. Somewhere along the line, they changed that and they started giving us cloth, treaty cloth.

And last month [September 2009] our shipment arrived here at Onondaga, from that Canandaigua Treaty. And it arrived in all of the other Haudenosaunee nations. So that treaty is still in effect. We still get those annuities from those treaties. And Oneida got their cloth also, so the treaty is still in effect in Oneida.

So again, the Sherrill Decision is violating treaties and the Constitution. Therefore it is invalid, illegal, and unconstitutional. And it's important for our young people to know these things. That's why I'm explaining this now.

And it's also important for the Oneida people to go back and look at their history and see what can be done about the Supreme Court.

Now Larry EchoHawk was here at Onondaga last month. And he explained what nation he came from, his clan, and his name. And his position in the Department of the Interior. And he said, "One of the things that we have to do is we have to change what the Supreme Court is doing. Because they're making decisions against our people. And they're taking away our rights."

Now he didn't have a solution. He didn't give us a solution. He just mentioned the fact that the Supreme Court was wrong in making their decision. So I went up to him and I said, "I appreciate what you said, and I'm of the opinion that the Sherrill Decision violated the Constitution of the United States in article 2 and article 3."

He said, "Correct, and it violates article 6."

I said, "That's right." So we're in agreement, you know, that the Supreme Court is wrong. How we change that is yet to be determined. But we're looking to see how we can do that.

Because the Supreme Court decision in Sherrill is based upon the Doctrine of Discovery* set up by a church in 1452. Now an opinion of the church is not law. But that Doctrine of Discovery is now in the laws and it's being used, used against the Oneidas. It was used against the Cayugas. And I don't know who else it was used against. But there's a possibility that anytime a nation puts in a land claim, the Doctrine of Discovery will be used against them.

Since I first wrote the above concerns, the Sherrill Decision has affected the Onondaga land claim. It, too, has been dismissed.

And I understand, you know, that when they set up the United States, they separated church and state. And they said that they wouldn't have them together. And after all of these years, I guess that part of history is

* The Discovery Doctrine is a concept of public international law expounded by the US Supreme Court in a series of decisions. The doctrine has been primarily used to support decisions invalidating or ignoring Aboriginal possession of land in favor of colonial or post-colonial governments.

forgotten or ignored. One of the two. And that Supreme Court is ruling on an opinion of a church. Not a law: it's something somebody said.

We've had these kinds of problems all along. In 1948, the United States decided they were going to pass a law giving criminal jurisdiction to the state of New York over the Haudenosaunee. And we went down and said, "You can't do this. You can't pass these laws. If you do, the state of New York is going to come and tax us."

In 1948 it was criminal jurisdiction; in 1950 it was civil jurisdiction. And civil jurisdiction, [as] it is understood by the state, carries the authority to tax. Because that's a civil matter.

And then the government at that time said, "No, this is not about taxes. This is about opening up our court system so that you can use our courts to settle your disputes. When you have a dispute with the city or county or something, our courts are open for you. You can use them."

But in 1958, Edward Best, attorney general for the state of New York, stood up in a room in Albany and said, "It's my opinion that the New York Indians should be paying taxes." And so that started our tax fight—based on one man's opinion, not a court case. It was not ruled in court. But the court cases that we do have are from Judge Gorman and Judge Henry, which say sales tax laws in Onondaga Territory—which would mean all of the other Haudenosaunee territories—are invalid, illegal, and unconstitutional. Because they don't have the right to come into our territory.

And in 1971 and 1972, we argued with the state on Route 81, which goes through our territory. It's a federal highway. And the state put an injunction on us and said we couldn't go up on that road and protest their addition of a third lane. It was called a "safety lane."

Well, we went through our lawyer and we said, "You know, we were never in court. How can they do this stuff without us being in court?" So the lawyer went up to Utica and talked to the judge up there, James O'Donnell. He said, "You ruled without my client being in court. You've got to reopen the case." And so he did. And we presented our position on sovereignty, treaties, and so forth. Judge O'Donnell then ruled in 1972 that the New York State Department of Transportation did "not have the power of eminent domain" in the territory of the Onondagas. And they were told to stop work on Route 81 and remove themselves.

That court decision was never appealed and it still stands today; it's still in effect. Which clearly states that New York does not have any jurisdiction in our territory because of who we are. We're a sovereign nation with territory that is not part of the United States, is not part of the state of New York. And the laws that are passed are for the United States. And the state laws that are passed are for the state of New York. And since we're not part of the United States and we're not part of the state of New York, none of these laws that they pass apply in our territory.

That's why it's important for our young people to look at these treaties and the *intent* of the treaties.

I know that what I'm presenting is very new to you. Because I know that New York State does not present the history of the relationship between the Haudenosaunee (and the various nations of the Haudenosaunee), the relationships between us and the United States. You don't know about these things.

Well, I have talked about how we explained our system of government to the colonists. And I knew that we went down to Philadelphia, but I didn't have a date. So Bob Venables went in on his computer [and] researched it. He came back. He said, "Irv, you were down in Philadelphia in 1744. You ended up in Lancaster, Pennsylvania. And this is where you presented the Constitution and the bylaws of the Haudenosaunee." And he handed me this piece of paper.

And I said, "Wow, how 'bout that!"

So anyway, these documents are available. And because I know that you've never heard about this before, you may be saying, "Well how can he make those kinds of statements?"

I can make these statements because of my oral history. I am not a citizen of the United States. I am not a citizen of the state of New York. I'm seventy-eight years old.* I've never voted and I don't intend to vote because I am a citizen of the Onondaga Nation. Therefore I have a different status and I don't want to be a citizen of the United States. Too many rules, too many restrictions. I'm a free person. . . .

* As of November 13, 2007.

One of these days, maybe we'll be able to settle this so that the treaties will be honored and the obligations will be met. And then we can have peace and friendship, as designed in the first treaty that was made in the early 1600s between the Dutch and the Haudenosaunee.

And that treaty is still in effect. And Timothy Pickering, spokesman for the United States at Canandaigua in 1794 stated that he was negotiating "so that the chain of friendship would be brightened." So he understood that he was renewing his nation's obligations. And that's the treaty that I just spoke about.

So after all of those years, that treaty was mentioned again. He didn't give a date. All he said was, "the chain of friendship," referring to the Silver Covenant Chain, which is how it [the treaty] is known in English. In our language, it's Kahsweñhda², the Two Row Wampum Belt.

And on the website or whatever at Cornell University, those papers are there in their archives. So I thought it would be very educational for people to understand that the decision by the Supreme Court on Sherrill is illegal, invalid, and unconstitutional because of the treaties that we have, and because of what is stated in the Constitution under articles 2, 3, and 6. And Sherrill cannot tax the Oneidas as stated by the Supreme Court because they don't have jurisdiction there.

I think this is a very important part of history that our young people should understand. And to do research on it, the Constitution of the United States is available. All you need to do is obtain that and you can read articles 2, 3, and 6, and verify what I'm saying.

Reporters

I'd like to make a comment about those that interview people who win tro-phies, such as divers, marathon racers, or hundred-yard hurdlers. They're called reporters. And they're not divers, they're not runners, but they're right there at the finish line with their microphones. And they always seem to ask dumb questions to the people who win the race or the event.

And they'll say to the diver, "Well, what were you thinking about as you entered the water on your dive?" And, "What were you thinking about as you were approaching the finish line on this run that ended the marathon?" So they ask these questions that are really tough to answer. Sometimes the ones they interview don't have answers for them.

Anyway, my question is, "Who are these people, anyway, that ask these questions?" Now if I was a runner and I won a race and a reporter came up to me and said, "What were you thinking about as you were approaching the finish line?" my answer would be, "Well, I was thinking, if I win this race, what kind of dumb questions is that reporter going to ask me when I win?!"

The tree

Being at meetings with the environmental people, I've been asked, you know, how do we relate to the environment. And I say, "Well, we don't relate to the environment; we *are* the environment. We are one. We are the wind; we are the rain; we are the thunder."

So we refer to the thunder as our grandfather. It's part of us, part of the family. The sun is our brother. The moon is our grandmother. So the environment, and the winds and the rain and all that . . . and the trees are all part of us. And there's a total respect for that.

So someone said, "What do you mean?"

I said, "Well, this is my drum." Now this drum was made in 1975. My dad and I were holding classes down at the cookhouse on Saturday afternoons. And we did this for about three years. Every Saturday, we met. And we talked to the kids about who they were, what they were, what was expected of them as Haudenosaunee people. And we talked to them about what they were supposed to do with that.

So one of them asked if they could make drums. And my dad had just received seventy-five skins, deerskins. So he said to me, "We've got plenty of skins to make drums." He said, "We can do that."

And I said, "All right. So next Saturday, we'll make drums."

So the next Saturday we showed up at the cookhouse with a saw, and tobacco. And we got all the kids together, put them in the car, and we drove up to the south end. And there, we went into the woods.

When we got into the woods, we looked around at the various trees and we picked out a cedar tree that was just nice. It had a diameter of about five inches around the base, so it would make a nice circumference for a drum. So we built a fire and we burned tobacco for the tree. And we explained to the tree that we were taking its life, but the tree would live on, spiritually, because it would provide music for the ceremonies of the Onondaga Nation.

And we thanked the tree for being there and for the things that he had done. He provided shade, he provided a home for the birds, and he had done everything he was supposed to do. And now he was going to do something else: he was going to provide us with the material to make a drum. So he would not end his duties when we took his life, but he would continue on performing because he would be providing us with the music for our ceremonies. He would be part of that.

And so we burned tobacco, explained that to the tree and then we cut the tree down. And then we cut the tree up into sections, six inches each. We came back to the cookhouse and we hollowed out the trees—the sections that we had, hollowed them out. Then we stretched a deerskin over each of them and made drums, water drums.

So this drum that I have was made in 1975. After I finished making the drum, I took the drum to every ceremony that we've had since then, since 1975. So for the last thirty-five years this drum has been in all the ceremonies at Onondaga, doing exactly what we said it would do. So the tree has lived on, providing music for our ceremonies at the longhouse. And it has done a fine job at it.

And it got so that they wouldn't start the ceremonies unless my drum was there. And they would say, "Where is the drum?" So I would have to go home and get the drum and bring it. And then we would have our ceremony. But they wouldn't start it unless the drum was there.

My drum was there right up until the time that Tracy Shenandoah took over the duty of taking care of the rattles for the ceremonies, which I had been doing. When he took that, he also took on the responsibility of providing the drum. And I think his drum was also one of those that we made from that tree. So the tree was still there. After my drum stopped, another drum took over. But it was from the same tree. And it's still there, today. In fact, I saw the drum in the longhouse just the other day, waiting for the next ceremony.

But this is how we connect to everything. We pay respect, our respect to the tree for what it has done, up to the time we took its life. And we give thanks to the tree for continuing on by providing music for our ceremonies. So the tree still lives. It has lived on since 1975.

This is all part of the concept of our closeness to the environment. And since we knew that there was a life there, when we cut the tree down to make a drum, we had a ceremony. We burned tobacco for the tree, and explained what we were doing, and why we were taking its life. But it would be used and it's still used today.

So the spirit and life of the tree lives on and will continue to live on in the concept that we have, that all the environment has a life: trees, plants, grass, flowers, whatever. Whatever's out there in the environment has a life and is a part of us.

Very important matter, because in the mandates of the Haudenosaunee and in the nations of the Haudenosaunee, we are required to make sure that the trees continue. And we make sure that the plants and the medicines continue on, that we have here today. That they continue on into the future for the seven generations. So that our great-grandchildren will be able to enjoy the same things that we have today.

And that duty was given to us by the Peacemaker over 2,000 years ago. And we still live by these rules and regulations that were given to us. And that's why it's so important that when we go out and take the life of a plant or a medicine, we burn tobacco for that and we explain to the plant, "You are here for a purpose. Your purpose is to heal people and help them in their need. And the time now has come for you to do this, so we are going to take your life. And you are going to go and you are going to assist Dehatgahdoñs to continue on with his life, spiritually and emotionally and whatever . . . traditionally. But your life will live on in the medicine that you provide to make him healthy."

So it's very important that we understand this and pass this information on to our children so that they will continue to do this. And when they go out after medicine to help somebody out, they never take the first one; they always look for another. And that's the one they pick. And that's the one they burn tobacco for and explain that they're taking the life of the plant so that it can continue on with what it's supposed to do, to help somebody else. This concept is very important for our people to understand. As one of the spiritual and cultural leaders of the Onondaga

Nation, it's my job to make sure that my sons understand it, so they can tell *their* children. So that the tradition travels on. Now this has been going on for over 2,000 years, and it's still here.

And if you talk to the various other nations, and the medicine people, this is what you'll find out, that this is still there with the other nations. That's why I mentioned Jake Swamp earlier, because in one of his presentations this is what he said. When he goes out after medicine, he never picks the first one that he sees; he always looks for other ones. And those are the ones he picks and those are the ones he burns tobacco for.

This is something that *we* do. But I notice that in your world, people will come in and they will clear-cut. They will cut every tree in a parcel of land and not have one ceremony for any one of those trees. And think nothing of all those lives that they took. And because we think this way, it's impossible for us to walk alone in the woods.

I heard a person say, "Well, I took a walk in the woods, alone."

I said, "No, you weren't alone. You cannot walk in the woods alone because there are the lives of all the trees that are with you. And the lives of all of the plants and the medicines that are in the forest are also with you. Millions of lives. All the animals: the deer, bear, raccoons, chipmunks, squirrels, and the birds are all there with you."

So you cannot walk alone in the woods. Not in our society, anyway, you can't. Maybe the newcomers think, though, that they can in theirs because so many of them disregard all of those trees and all of those animals. They don't seem to think of them as we do. So perhaps that is why they feel no remorse about cutting all the trees in an area.

Not only in this country, but [also] in South America. I met a Yanomami Native from Brazil. He told me that he was thirty-five years old before he met a white man, and that was just a couple of years ago. So he was around thirty-eight years old when I met him. He said that these people have come into their territory and they have cut down *every* mahogany tree in the area.

And to do so, they had to do some other stuff. And what they're doing is polluting the Amazon River. So the fish are now polluted. And the Yanomani people are not able to do what they used to do a few years ago. And this is just within a couple of years that these people have come in.

But they have no feelings towards these trees. It's just . . . it's a commercial item where they can make money.

And we don't look at a tree as a commercial item where you can make money. We look at a tree as a part of our society; it's part of us. So it's important that we give thanks to the tree for doing his duty.

I said to some young people I was talking to, I said, "We were all given duties, way back when. The tree was given duties. We were given duties. A tree was given a duty to produce apples. So every year since that time, this tree has produced apples for the people. And I have never heard an apple tree say, 'You know, I'm tired of doing this. I'm not going to do this anymore.'"

But I hear people say that. You know, "I'm tired of doing what I'm supposed to be doing."

We can't do that. We have to be like the apple tree. Every year we do the same thing, over and over again, because that's what our duties are, to provide for tomorrow what we have today. Very important that the people who listen to this or read this understand this. Look around you and see what's here, and see what you want to preserve for your great-grandchildren. And then you work towards preserving that.

When I was a young boy here at Onondaga, when I used to go hunting I would take a glass or a container with me so that when I came across a stream of water, I would be able to dip my glass or cup into the water and take a drink. And today you can't do that because of pollution.

But that's not how it's supposed to be. So we are working with the DEC and the EPA to try to restore Onondaga Lake and its watershed to be like it was when the Europeans came into our territory. Because you could drink the water. There were animals here at that time that are no longer here.

My children have never seen the stuff that I've seen—never experienced it and never will. And I have not experienced some of the stuff that my dad has. It's gone by, and I don't know how we get back to that time, but it's something we have to think about. The preservation of today, for tomorrow, is a very important concept to think about.

The house that you're living in isn't built for today; it's built for tomorrow. So it has to be strong. It has to be able to withstand the winds, the rains, and whatever's coming. So if you think of things in that manner, it changes your concept of your position on Mother Earth, and your relationship to all of the things that are here.

It's very important that people realize that this is a commitment that was made by your ancestors when they sat with us in the early 1600s, and agreed to come into our territory and live under our laws. Our laws are just that simple. Simple, but hard to follow. *You will preserve what's here today, for tomorrow.* So think of what you're doing. And when you make a decision, make sure that you're deciding on the future.

I have a lot of people coming to my house because I'm secretary of the nation. And these people are looking for ways to restore themselves as Potawatomi, Lakota, Blackfoot, or something because their grandmother decided that she didn't want to be a Native anymore. And so she removed herself from the rolls, removed herself completely from any connection with Native people, her people.

And she did such a fine job that her grandchildren now cannot reconnect. So she made a decision back there whenever it was, that her grandchildren would not be Native. And her grandchildren are not too happy with that decision. Because they want to be Native. They've heard about it and they say, "Well, I have Native blood in me and that's what I want to be. I would like to know everything I can about who I am and what I'm supposed to be doing as a Native person."

But their grandmother was so good at what she was doing, she severed those ties and they're unable to reconnect. So what you do today has an effect on your grandchildren. And you have to think about that when you're doing things. Remember when you're doing something, say, "Well, how will my grandchildren react when they find out that this is what I did?"

And they won't be able to ask me—because I'm gone—"Grandma, why did you do that?" Or, "Grandpa, why did you do that?" Because you did that, this is what's happening now, today. You've taken this away from us. And you really didn't have the right to take this away from me because it wasn't yours to take away.

It's a concept of who we are and what we are and what we're about that seems to be totally different in my world than it is in yours. But it's something that I like to talk about so that in the future you will think this way.

And maybe we can make this a better world. And maybe we can make this a world where we have peace and no wars. Because when we joined together, we were told, at that meeting, that we, the people of the day, have the duty of preserving for tomorrow so that we will have grandchildren with the same kind of concepts and ideas that we have. And in order to do that, you have to think that way: the seven generations ahead. And you have to think, what will be the effect of that? What will my grandchildren say if I remove this? And will they say, "You shouldn't have done that"?

So we have to think that way. The message that we received was: what you are doing and how you are living is not how you're supposed to be living. You should not be arguing and fighting with each other. The Creator gave you a mind, a brain to think with. And he said that with that brain, you should be able to sit down and resolve your disputes without war.

It's a simple statement, but if followed, there would be no wars and the whole world would be at peace. There would be respect for each other as a people, the different languages, the different religions, different governments. And the respect for each other would then enable the people to sit down and resolve a dispute without going to war. So we would have peace. And that's the message that we received. And so for the last 2,000 years this is what we've been taught. And this is what we teach.

So when I go out to universities, this is what I mention, that there should be no wars in this world. And if we did what we were told to do, there wouldn't be any wars.

The hummingbirds

To show our connection to the environment further, to show how the environment and us are together, I would like to tell you of an incident that happened some years ago. You may be interested in how our connection is, but the environmentalists are also interested in our relationship to the environment, how we relate to it. And so they set up a meeting in Tucson, Arizona, and they invited spiritual leaders from many of the different Native nations: Thomas Banyacya, the Seminoles from Florida, Jake Swamp from the Mohawk Nation, and me. And many environmentalists and people from the DEC and the EPA were there.

So we arrived. And these people wanted to learn how to connect to the environment like we do. I *think* that that's what they were trying to do. Anyway, we got to the meeting and Monday we spent introducing ourselves.

And so we formed a circle that was orchestrated by Tom Banyacya of the Hopis, who in 1948 was made spiritual leader for the Hopi nation. And he would be the one to go out and tell about the prophecies of the Hopi nation. So in the 1950s he came to Onondaga and he met with us and we discussed prophecies and ceremonies. But when this meeting took place, Tom was there, Jake, and I. And Tom took over and he said, "When the Hopis have a meeting such as this, we always form a circle and we call it a sacred circle." He said, "So everybody sit in a circle." So we formed a big circle.

And on Monday, all of the people—the white people who were there—stood up and introduced themselves. And being who they are, they also included where they went to school and what degrees they had: they were so and so; they had a bachelor's degree; they had a master's degree. And some had PhDs in environmental sciences from different universities throughout the United States.

And then, after they got through, the Native people stood up and introduced themselves. And it was real quick, like "I'm Jake Swamp from the Mohawk Nation." "I'm Billy Two Rivers from the Mohawk Nation." "I'm so-and-so from whatever nation." It got around to me and I just told them "I am Chief Irving Powless, the chief of the Beaver Clan of the Onondaga Nation." And that was it, that's how *we* introduced ourselves. So it was very quick, how it went around the circle. So that was Monday.

So Tuesday we sat and we talked about the environment and so forth—Tuesday, Wednesday, and Thursday. And Thursday was our final day. So it was in the afternoon when Tom said, "Well," he said, "we've been sitting here for four days, and I want to review what has happened."

Oh, before I go there, I want to tell you this. A Hawaiian was there, and when the Hawaiian got to the meeting, I watched him as he walked away. And he went over the hill and he disappeared. He was gone for about fifteen minutes and then he came back. So when he stood up and introduced himself, he said he was from the Hawaiian Islands. And he said, "When I got here, I took a little walk," he said, "and when I got over to a place over here, there was a big argument between a blackbird and a bluebird. And the blackbird said, 'You don't belong here. Go on home.' And the bluebird said, 'No, he was walking on lava. The same substance that is at his home. And because he's walking on the same substance here as he does at home, he's welcome and he belongs here.'"

He said, "The bluebird won the argument." He said, "So I'm here. And I'm glad to be here." He said, "I'm glad that you invited me. And it's really good to see all of these people here, all of the Native people from across the country."

So anyway, we had the four days of meetings and we talked about the environment. And so Tom was closing the meeting. He said, "We opened the meeting with a thank you to all of the things that the Creator has given to us. And Jake Swamp did that in the language of the Mohawks. And then he explained in English what he said." He said, "So we close our meetings with the same Thanksgiving. And so if we can have Jake do that again, we will then close the meeting."

So Jake stood up and he closed the meeting. And after he closed the meeting, then Tom said, "Well," he said, "now that the meeting is closed, let's give a little review of what happened while we were sitting here talking about the environment."

"Before we started the meeting," he said, "we had two Lakota people come and they sat in the middle of the circle and they had two bundles with them. And they opened up their bundles, and as they opened their bundles, they sang seven songs."

He said,

And we noticed that there were seven eagles circling above us. And that's an indication to us that the Creator is watching us and he approves of what we're doing. And that what we're doing is correct. He sent the eagles to tell us this.

And when they finished singing their songs, they had opened up their bundles. And in each bundle was a pipe. And so they took the ingredients out of their pouches and put them into the pipes and lit the pipes. And then they passed the pipes around the circle so that we all smoked a pipe.

And while we did this, the Lakotas stuck into the ground a stick. Hanging from the stick was an eagle feather. And there was a medicine wheel made out of porcupine quills—black, red, yellow, and white. And so as we sat here in the circle . . . one day, four butterflies came into our circle and flew around the inside of it. There were four butterflies: one was black, one was white, one was yellow, and one was red—the four colors of the sacred circle. . . .

And as we sat here, one of the days . . . a bluebird came in and sat in that tree. And the bluebird sang to us, confirming the story that the Hawaiian told us, that the bluebird said it was okay for him to be here. So the bluebird came into our circle. He came in, flew around our circle and sat in that tree and confirmed the story of the Hawaiian.

Then, as we sat, a hummingbird came into our circle. And the hummingbird flew around the inside of the circle and left. A couple of minutes later, he came back into our circle, flew around the circle, and this time he went over and he put his beak on the eagle feather. And then he went out of the circle and came back in again. This time he went over to the medicine wheel and he put his beak on the medicine wheel. Then he left again and he flew back into the circle. He flew around the inside of the circle and then he stopped in front of that lady, sitting over there. And he hovered right in front of her. And he put his beak on her nose. And then he left.

But that's what we have seen, while we were sitting here. And so we want to thank everybody for coming . . . and if there's anything else that anybody wants to add, you can do so now.

I raised my hand. And so Tom said, "Irv Powless from the Onondaga Nation has something to add to this."

So I stood up. And I said, "Well, we were all coming down here," I said, "and I was leaving Sunday. So Sunday afternoon, I was sitting with my family telling about going to Tucson, Arizona on environmental issues." I said, "And while we talked, a hummingbird came in and flew to me and then to my wife and then to my daughter. And my granddaughter was over on the slide, playing. And the hummingbird went over and sat on the clothesline and watched my granddaughter as she went down the slide, and then flew away. But the hummingbird was there to tell us, you know, that we would have a good trip," I said.

"And now," I said, "here we are, 2,000 miles away from my house. And into the circle comes a cousin of that hummingbird that came to us. And he came into our circle, circled around and touched the feather, the medicine wheel, and that woman. The hummingbird was welcoming us to his territory. And he was also sending a message back to his cousin that said we had arrived all right and we were here, having a good meeting. So it's very important, you know, that you understand that this is who we are and this is what happens when we have these kinds of meetings," I said. "Thank you." And I sat down.

And Tom said, "Well, that's very nice," he said, "to have that portion of the story added, and to have the hummingbird sanction our meeting. And with that we'll say goodbye and thank you, everybody, for coming. And maybe we'll see each other in the future." And the meeting ended that way.

It's so great to be able to witness the response from the Creator as he sends us messages or signals that what we're doing is correct. So when the hummingbird came to me in my house and then came to our circle in Arizona, that was a big event for me, to have that hummingbird come. And not only the hummingbird, but the bluebird, who confirmed the Hawaiian's story.

Now the environmentalists from the DEC and the EPA came to learn how we relate to the environment. And they watched for four days and they saw what happened. And if they think that now they have seen this, that they're going to be able to hold a circle like ours, and that's going to happen? It's not going to happen with them because they don't have the spiritual connection to the environment that we do.

It would be interesting to see what those people wrote in their report about what happened at their meeting or what they said when they came back and reported to their committees or to their bosses about the meeting they had with the "environmental Indian people." Because that was quite an event to be part of and to witness, and to have the Creator send these messages to us that said, "You're doing right. You're working to preserve and you're teaching. And that's what you're supposed to do."

Anyway, I thought this would be a good way to finish the book, to show that we *are* the environment and the environment is part of us. And wherever we go, whatever we do, the environment is with us and lets us know. Sometimes with just a soft breeze, as I mentioned before on another topic. I told you about the time I sat and I watched the trees move. And by the wind in the trees, they informed me that it was going to rain. And that following morning, it rained, just like the wind said it was going to do. So our connection to the environment and what's around us is very close.

And, let's see, I've told you about my drum and I still have that drum. And for all of these years, I still have it. I still use it. I use it when I sing the ancient songs that were given to us. And it's so . . . hmm . . . I don't know, I don't have the words to explain what it is, the feeling that you get when these things happen, when the bluebirds come, when the hummingbirds come, or the butterflies come, and let you know that what you are doing is correct.

There's no way of explaining what that feeling is like, to know that you are a part of a big force that is looking after Mother Earth and the things that are here for our benefit. And as we continue on our life, we will teach our kids, our children, to have the same relationship so that they can pass it on. And seven generations from now, the same stories will be told, and the same things will happen: birds will show up; butterflies will show up, to let us know that they are watching us and we're doing the things that we're supposed to do.

Closing

There are many other instances that bring up the question, "Who are these people anyway?" and I believe I haven't covered them all. So at this time, since we have finished writing, you have the ability now to think about these things that would bring up the question and add it to the book so that it makes the book more complete.

And this book covers a lot of territory, but it's what I think is *very* necessary for my people to remember, that we are Onkwehonwe. We're Onoñda'gegá' and we're Haudenosaunee. And here is the priority, the *top* priority, of us as a people: it is to continue on the ways of our people, the things that the Creator has given to us: our songs, our dances, our foods, our way of life, so that our grandchildren will be saying the same things that our ancestors said.

And we've done this. I've made speeches, and then I've read the words of our ancestors. And they're almost identical in presentation.

And to the non-Native people, we would like to, at this time, say, "We'll see you again sometime." And think of peace and how do we achieve peace in this world? But we start with respect. If we have respect for each other, we can then sit down and respect the differences that we have in such a manner that we can resolve disputes without war.

Ne' tho di' neñyohdik ne' oñgwa'nigoñhä·'. Let us put our minds together as one and give thanks to all the things that the Creator has given us. And when we do this, let our minds be that way.

Da· ne' thoh. That is all I have to say.